ENDORSEMENTS

"Niccie is an exciting new leader whose compassion and conviction comes through in equal measure in *Awaking the Living Legacy*. *Awaking the Living Legacy* provides the sorts of probing questions and toolkit of next steps to jumpstart spiritual maturation in its readers. Both theologically rooted and highly applicable, this work will become an important conversation partner for anyone who is seeking fresh direction in life's journey toward legacy."

Pastor Tim Breen
Lead Pastor, Orange City, Iowa

"Niccie is compassionately driven in her mission as a leader and catalyst for spiritual growth through Christ, sharing her compelling and authentic story, as well as some of her most popular coaching tools and life applications for you to immediately put into practice. *Awaking the Living Legacy* is a timely solution to today's overwhelming stress and demands of this busy world."

Tanya Mundo, LCPC, PCC, NCC
Design Your World

"What the world needs now is more people who have faith in God. Niccie Kliegl shares her personal and engaging faith journey which she reminds us is accessible for anyone. *Awaking the Living Legacy* is an encouraging guide by a great coach to successful living."

Pastor Harlan VanOort
Pastor at City Church
Denver, Colorado

AWAKING THE LIVING LEGACY

NICCIE KLIEGL

AUTHOR ACADEMY elite

Printed in the United States of America
2016 First Edition
Paperback ISBN- 978-1-943526-83-3
Hardcover ISNB- 978-1-943526-82-6
Library of Congress Control Number- 2016914330
Published by Author Academy Elite
P.O. Box 43, Powell, OH 43035
www.AuthorAcademyElite.com

The Internet addresses in this book are accurate at the time of publication. They are provided as a resource. Niccie Kliegl and the publisher do not endorse them or vouch for their content or permanence.

To protect the privacy of those who have shared their stories with the author, some details and names have been changed.

DEDICATION

I would like to dedicate *Awaking the Living Legacy* to my sister Caprice.

Your deeply rooted love for our Father and your faith journey is a testament to those who read these pages. You are an inspiration to me and for all who hope to abide in the 'Living Legacy.' Thank you for your sisterly love that never fails.

I love you dear Sister,
Light the way

AWAKING THE LIVING LEGACY
STUDY GUIDE

For Small Groups or Workshops

Small group and workshop leaders, be sure to download the The Living Legacy, Life Transformation Study Guide. Broken down into just six sessions, you and your group will work through a systematic process for approaching life within the strength, ease and support of our Heavenly Father.

Awaking the Living Legacy ignites personal reflection and growth through it's study questions and interactive processes. I made The Living Legacy, Life Transformation Study Guide FREE and applicable, to work independently or in groups of all sizes.

Download @... nicciekliegl.com

Contents

FOREWORD

A ripple effect occurs when one action results in a continued effect.

Throughout history, big and small acts of kindness and destruction have rippled through our nation. We do our best to be part of the good, and steer clear of the bad. We jam-pack our lives with efforts to gain success, and to leave our mark on this world. We give to our careers, go the extra mile as a parent, pray for our marriages, and seek out best friends...so why, then, do we often feel lost, misdirected and empty?

Author Niccie Kliegl passionately shares how to remove yourself from the path of destruction and into the wake of greatness.

Awaking the Living Legacy teaches a systematic approach for gaining clarity and insight to who you are, and who you are designed to be. Niccie then takes you on a journey of healing and growth that awakens you to all God has to offer and then what He wants in return.

Awaking the Living Legacy was inspired by Niccie's passion to infuse faith into the daily lives of those she coaches, leads, speaks to and writes for. Niccie has broken her chapters down into six of her most sought after coaching programs. Each of these six areas are reviewed with the same systematic approach, teaching you a process for handling your days in a way that results in health, wellness, and abundance that only God can provide.

Kary Oberbrunner
CEO of Redeem the Day and Igniting Souls
Author of *Elixir Project, Day Job to Dream Job,*
The Deeper Path, and *Your Secret Name*

PREFACE

From the moment I decided to write this book I knew I would be writing for readers at varying places of their faith journey. I understand and appreciate how each person has their own journey. Everyone's faith is in a unique place that only they and God know.

No one journey is better than the next. In fact, we are designed to be walking in faith together and sharing this good news with others, knowing that along our journey we will encounter some who are excited or maybe tentative in their new faith, others who are firm and unwavering from a deeply tested faith, and others yet found in many places between the two.

I call on each reader to do just this. Evaluate the place you are at in your faith, embrace the place you are in and the place your neighbor is in. Learn from those who have much to offer, and give to anyone who finds that you have something they may need in their journey.

~ My prayer ~
Dear Heavenly Father, let the hearts, minds, and souls of those who read these pages, turn the last with a sweeter smile and a more deeply committed life of passion to "love and do."
In the name of Jesus, glory be to God, Amen.

ACKNOWLEDGMENTS

To my Heavenly Father, for guiding me and leading my steps. I am truly rooted in you and your way. I humbly wait for the next steps of my God-given life, knowing I am not yet prepared, but when partnered with you, I always will be able.

To my husband Jeff, and your unwavering support. You made writing *Awaking the Living Legacy* possible. Few know how much you have been a part of their success as they go to live out their God-given life purpose and abide in the legacy Jesus left behind for them.

To Caprice, my sister, for countless hours of editing and encouragement. Thank you for all your hard work and sound advice. You always know just what I need.

To Shirley, my loving mother. I am so grateful to have you in my corner. Thank you for your late nights of support, cheering me on, and for being my prayer warrior.

To all of my supporting friends and family members! A special thank you goes to Christi Vander Voort with her keen marketing sense, Tricia Wiese and Cheryl Bakker for hours of honest editing and encouragement, JoAnn, Harlan, Missy, and Pastor Tim who gave so much in kindness, prayers and support to make this book happen.

To Tanya Mundo, my Life Coach Certification instructor and mentor, who inspired me from the beginning to be true to who I am and who I am designed to be...sound familiar Tanya? She is a highly successful and sought after coach herself who desires nothing more than to see others rise up. Had my instructor been anyone else, my path would have taken a different direction and Tanya, I just cannot thank you enough!

To Kary Oberbrunner, appointed by God to help me on this path to help others. Kary is my Author Coach and mentor. This book simply would not be without him. He leads with grace and skill, wanting nothing more than to give and serve. Thank you for investing in me. I will use your knowledge wisely.

Introduction

I am a Speaker, Author, Certified Life Coach and Registered Nurse. The last twenty some years of my working life I was a nursing leader, and found team building and leading others to reach their highest potential to be my passion.

I have witnessed individuals over and over again rise up and make huge transformations in their health, relationships, goals, and more importantly in their whole lives.

As I broke off in 2015 to build my own company, *Fulfill Your Legacy* Life Coaching, I did it with many of the same principles I have used for years with patients, team members, and peer leaders. Being the sole proprietor of *Fulfill Your Legacy*, I have been able to more intentionally infuse faith into this process of life transformation, and I am in awe of the strength, success, and abundance that my clients are gaining when faith is at the foundation of their growth.

It brings me such joy to know this book will give each reader an opportunity to learn the processes I use when coaching my clients to deepen their place with God, to come to know their life purpose, and to gain a life of health and abundance that they never dreamed possible.

You will find six parts to this book. Each part is a fundamental practice of Fulfill Your Legacy's coaching. Each of these six parts are broken down into four chapters. The chapters pattern an essential process, The 4C Approach, to Faith Infused Living.

The first chapter of each part is – "Consider the Problem." Here we will look at the problems that hold us back from the legacy Jesus left behind for each and every one of us. The second chapter of each part is - "Consider the 'Word.'" Here we will learn to look to the 'Word' for answers to our everyday concerns and our biggest trials. The third chapter of each part is - "Consider the Gifts." This is where we consider what is available to us as we cling to what we know is true and what is written. Fourth, and last, is - "Consider the Choice." After we have gained all of the wisdom we can get from the previous steps, we will be ready to make an informed wise choice.

You will also find topics highlighted in boxes to the side of the page for a deeper look at various transformational thoughts.

I have made an optional study guide to use independently or in groups, to dive deeper into these processes of faith-infused living and life transformation.

Free Study Guide found at...

nicciekliegl.com

May the Lord make your love increase and overflow for each other and for everyone else, just as ours does for you.

1 Thessalonians 3:12

PART 1

I AM HIS &
HE IS MINE

THE PROBLEM

CHAPTER 1

DO YOU KNOW YOUR LIFE PURPOSE?

I AM HIS AND HE IS MINE

I Am His & He Is Mine...

THE PROBLEM

DO YOU KNOW YOUR LIFE PURPOSE?

Through this story I share with you how I came to know that I am His and He is mine. This very story set me on a path to fulfill my life purpose. It wasn't until I allowed myself to be claimed by Him, and He by me, that my purpose began to unfold. This is when you will begin to see your life purpose take root in a way that feeds your soul, shares the true light, and grows in the glory of our Almighty. Does being claimed by God help manifest our true life purpose?

"You are a CHOSEN race...a people for God's own possession,"
1 Peter 2:9 English Standard Version (ESV)

My story is like many others. I was raised as a Christian, I knew the laws, and I did fairly well following them. The Holy Spirit lived in me from an age so young I barely remember.

Some might wonder just what that felt like or how I knew the Holy Spirit lived in me. First of all, I believe the Holy Spirit dwells in the hearts of many children, and more specifically, before we learn to doubt.

I did not understand the important role of my pastor, Pastor Anderson from Mason City, Iowa, had until I began studying the Bible. I had no idea Acts 8:14-17 (seen below) was even a Bible verse. What I did know as a child, is that I loved going up to the front of the church during communion. Any child, not yet confirmed, was invited to go up during communion. Instead of receiving communion, my pastor laid his hand on our heads and reminded us of our acceptance by grace as he gave us God's blessing, regardless of all our confessed sins.

After blessing each one of us, in a booming and reassuring voice, he would repeat to us all, "May the Lord bless you and keep you. May the Lord's face shine upon you and be gracious unto you. May He lift up his countenance upon you and give you peace."

These spoken words were 'heavy' and came to me in more of a physical form, each time working in me. They were like water and sun feeding my soul, giving me life and energy that I recognized without anyone telling me I should. It simply was. I couldn't have been more than five when I learned to give myself to this love and acceptance, because the more I let the words sink into me, the more peace and energy returned to me.

I was baptized as an infant. But children are losing their innocence early these days and having a relationship with God, the Father, and the Holy Spirit as a child should be fostered. When I confessed my sins, and believed that they were forgiven, and as my pastor laid his hands on me – I felt the truth of Acts 8:14-17 gifting me with the Holy Spirit each Sunday.

Now when the apostles at Jerusalem heard that Samaria had received the word of God, they sent to them Peter and John, who came down and prayed for them that they might receive the Holy Spirit, for he had not yet fallen on any of them, but they had only been baptized in the name of the

Lord Jesus. Then they laid their hands on them and they received the Holy Spirit. Acts 8:14-17 ESV

Now today, as we are baptized it is done in the name of God the Father, Son, and Holy Spirit. But I am talking about being in tune to the Holy Spirit and acknowledging his presence and work in our life.

I specifically referenced children earlier because children accept and believe naturally. This is why I feel strongly about getting our children into fabulous churches early in their lives. It wasn't like we were terribly active in church when I was young. Regular attendance to church was new to us and began when I was around five. So young moms and dads please know that just getting your kids into a good church can do wonders for a child's relationship with God, Jesus and the Holy Spirit. I had no idea I was developing a deep relationship with our God at that time. I'm not sure my family even knew. I didn't talk of it much - I simply thought it just was.

My mother tells me that from a very young age I would gravitate to those in need and would want to help them. This I now recognize as the Holy Spirit stirring in me, working in me, and building my gifts.

One particular example my mother reminded me of, while reading the rough draft of this book, was about a classmate of mine (I believe from second grade) whom I did not hang around with much, but tugged at my heart. My mother knew some of her story but never shared it with me until just the other day.

• • •

I recognized this classmate changing and it bothered me. I remember people making fun of her in school - over night it seemed she was changing. She started to smell of urine and her hair was uncombed and her clothes were dirty. I understood the distancing she got from our classmates but I knew something wasn't right. I befriended her and hated it at her house.

Her dad (or maybe step dad) was mean and scary. I remember her running to the window once as he came toward us, plopping onto the ground by the radiator, staring out the window. Then she began to urinate in her pants as she stared out the window. She wouldn't talk to me when I told her what she was doing. I wanted to help her but I couldn't. I wanted her to help herself but she couldn't.

I can still remember the smell of that man. It was an unfamiliar smell but distinct - I think alcohol and old smoke. I stood up as he walked toward us and told him to leave us alone. He laughed, and I remember noticing his yellow teeth and skinny frame. He didn't seem so big all the sudden. He seemed weak and I hollered for him to get away....AND HE DID.

I look back now, thinking that was nuts, a tiny child hollering at an unstable grown-up. I know now it never was me, it was the Holy Spirit who stood ground, who knew the power behind the voice that would come from my little frame. I never felt proud or strong and didn't even share this story until now, because until now I felt it wasn't mine to share.

Today I share it to be used, to spur thoughts and understanding of how God's power is used through the Holy Spirit.

We all have stories like these. We tuck them away, forget them, or write them off as chance and coincidence.

Today I want you to pull back the curtain on the power you have received in the past from the Holy Spirit, or the power you may have witnessed of another from the Holy Spirit. The power which will give you insight and ability to do things you would have otherwise avoided or overlooked.

Considering now that the Holy Spirit was stirring in me and working on me as I casually lived my days, I thought I was doing "just fine." Even into my adult years I did not understand all God wanted of me, and I did not know all I could be. I simply came to a place where I knew there was something more.

Feeling like there is something more for you to do?

Several incidents of my life increased my faith. I encountered people who heightened my sense of faith. And even at this minimal level of spiritual maturity, my faith was slowly growing. My problem was not a lack of desire to grow, but more so how to grow.

"Looking back, I see that God was always leading and directing me to more. He does not and will not give up on us as long as we are 'with' Him."

Consider the Problem: We don't always know how to find our life purpose or what it even is, in order to proceed.

As this story unfolds, you will see that you are part of my story, and by reading these pages He is reaching out to you... not willing to give up on even one of us and our continued growth in spirit and faith.

You are His & He is yours

Consider the Problem: Is your life purpose partnered with your faith?

Life purpose that is in line with our faith and in a place of continual growth, brings peace and contentment.

Do you know God's purpose for you?

Sharing your story is so valuable. When truly desiring to find your purpose in life, sharing stories helps you to see how God works differently in each person and how there is no perfect recipe for creating your specific purpose. Your God-given purpose is specific to you, unique and tucked inside you whether you are aware of it or not.

The Bible is chock full of stories, and Jesus used stories throughout his teaching because it worked. Here I will share my story with the hope of igniting another's faith to grow deeper, or to even spark for the first time.

This chapter is dedicated to you, the reader, to your purpose and level of faith, wherever it may be.

Some have always known God, Christ, and the Holy Spirit as well as understood their calling. Others think they know but there is a little twinge of doubt. Some absolutely have no idea but want to know, while others have no idea and give it very little thought. Even with this wide range of beliefs in Christ, my goal is for us each to be finding and deepening our faith each and everyday, living out what I call 'The Living Legacy.'

● ● ●

I was twenty-two years old and had just given birth to my first child, a darling girl named Raya. This was a fun time for Jeff, my husband, and I. We had become pregnant just three short months after getting married, and I had just completed nurse's training a few months before that. We lived in a trailer, which sat on a small lake in northwest Iowa.

It was a warm November day, and I remember feeling grateful for this wonderful fall weather. I had the front door open, and I was sitting directly across from it on the corner of our sectional couch. A large window was open next to the door, so the fall view cascaded in. As I held my daughter I didn't have a care in the world.

I was on my leave of absence, my new little house was all tidied up, my husband was at work, and my sweet baby girl had just finished feeding. I sat there taking in her smell along with those Autumn ones around me. Effortlessly, my mind moved to an overwhelming appreciation for our child. This appreciation couldn't help but accompany the most unconditional love I had ever experienced. I suppose I'd never loved someone more than myself before, or as much as I loved her- which is sort of hard for me to say because I loved my husband and my immediate family and even some friends so much. But this was definitely different.

This took me aback, and tears formed in my eyes...not out of guilt or pain but of amazement and gratitude. I had an overwhelming understanding of true and complete love. As my mind gained this understanding, which took root in my heart and soul, I was told, "THIS IS HOW MUCH I LOVE YOU." I didn't ask or even wonder. I didn't question who spoke to me...I didn't hear audible words...I heard meaning.

Yes, I know that is a strange concept-it's just that there are no words to put on such an insurmountable moment. I do not doubt for a minute that God speaks words to people, and you will come to understand God and His ways of communicating to you throughout these chapters. I am, however, explaining how He shared with me, His love for me, in a way that I understood throughout every cell in my body, every emotion I owned, every thought I possessed.

Words are good for us here in this worldly place, but maybe they are rather infantile and not necessary in the divine world. However, I'm getting ahead of myself. So as I heard the Lord my God confirm this deep love for me, thoughts then moved just as swiftly to my concern for God's love for Jesus, and how He managed to let one son die for another. I recognized how I was weak thinking I couldn't bear letting my sweet Raya die.

"No way, at no cost..."

As strange as it is, I didn't even get the words in my mind out, and He was answering before I finished. Almost in unison with my questions. And, again, not with words, but with more than words. I would best explain it as energy that almost seemed molecular. My thoughts seemed solid and shot between myself and God in whole form, which were answered wholly as well.

Sometime near this point, I let go of myself to go to Him. I wanted Him, and I wanted to know more about this love. In more than words He said 'yes' that he would tell me more and help me understand more. He assured me that as He shared, it would be painful, it would be hard for me to take, and that He was by me, with me, and I was able.

I trusted Him, and I opened myself up a little more. Like a river of energy, light, or equations, or something that's hard to explain, I learned so much about love and how true love is unconditional and what that REALLY means.

I felt broken hearted for God and Jesus dying, and I knew with this deeper knowledge that He absolutely did die for me...that He did die for you... every one of you! For any and everyone of you reading this book, as bold as I can be, I KNOW he died for you!

As I let this understanding sink in, I wept out of heartbreak. God revealed to me my sins. I truly felt some of the pain that I had caused in this world. It was so magnetic and real. I actually felt the hurts I caused others, and at that time I understood it was Jesus who carried that pain away for me. These incidents came faster than I could think, but I was keeping up.

This enlightenment took me to a new level of understanding my sin. Specific incidents flashed before me, and I felt the effects of those sins. I didn't even remember some of the experiences God revealed to me. But, I felt the effects of those too and knew then that, yes, I had done that too or caused that pain as well.

It was the little things that caught me off guard. This is why it is so important to confess even the transgressions you are unaware of doing. It was all of the comments, lack of assistance, contemptuous looks, or pride that I newly recognized as truly sinful...right along with the big ugly sins that I was completely aware of doing.

I wonder how long I sat there, and yet the whole encounter seemed timeless and all-consuming.

I remember acknowledging that the sadness, heartbreak, and pain I felt was in knowing Jesus bore all the weight of what "I" had done.

These feelings did NOT accompany guilt or shame. Here, in this worldly place, sin often accompanies guilt or shame, but there was nothing negative about my sin in this place. I asked

God about this, and I felt like He was sort of humored by my slowing things down, and yet He answered me.

I remember understanding at that point that we shouldn't waste God's love and Christ's gift by holding on to our sins and remaining in the effects of that sin.

Christ bears our sin as it is written, yet if we do not truly give it up and ask to be forgiven... we can let the sin grow and multiply here. Thereby adding to those Jesus had to bear. Oh, how human and heartbreaking this is for all. When we truly give our sin to Jesus, He bears it all...once and for all... so give it all away!

Consider the Problem: Do we hold on to pieces of our sin? Does keeping sin a secret to ourselves or others potentially lead to more sin? Does having a mind consumed with guilt and shame of a past sin limit the work Jesus, God and the Holy Spirit can do in us? Do we believe 1 Peter 3:18 and use this gift?

For Christ also suffered once for sins, the righteous for the unrighteous, to bring you to God. He was put to death in the body but made alive in the Spirit. 1 Peter 3:18

I again had to let go of myself and seek Him. As soon as I did the energy and light and understanding came back. I remember it took a little more strength or focus to come back. The first time it just happened, this time I may have begged in prayerful seeking, or needed with a deep desire, but it again returned from a place of love.

~ God is love and I deeply wanted this. ~

At this point I adopted a huge sense of accountability to do good, to be better. As quickly as I felt that, He then began to show me all the results of the loving and kind acts I had done. Just as before, they were not accompanied with sinful responses like self-pride or gloating. I remember feeling more acknowledged and reassured of His works through me during this time.

He helped me to know that even as I sin and pay for the consequences, He lives in me. I am not bad, un-loveable or wrong... the sin is. That is why He gave us Christ. As we give up our sin, that sin no longer lives in us and we are gifted an opportunity to be cleansed. This sets us up for being able to do more, love more and be more.

> **Consider the Problem:** Those who live in and of the world do not see or know him.
>
> *And I will ask the Father, and he will give you another advocate to help you and be with you forever—the Spirit of truth. The world cannot accept him, because it neither sees him nor knows him. But you know him, for he lives with you and will be in you.* John 14: 16-17

All this God wants for us. He wants us to do His work. The more clean and Christ-like we are, the more work we can do for Him. The Holy Spirit is also God. When Christ left this world we were given the Holy Spirit to dwell in us, if we so choose to believe and welcome God in. I understood the Triune God in a way I had never before.

I bet this is hard to hear if your position is to have only God, or to know no God. But, I do want you to hear that God too loves you and the Triune God (three in one: Jesus, God the Father, and the Holy Spirt) ...

~ died to have you with Him.~

He is waiting for us all. As we are working on sharing God's amazing love, forgiveness, and understanding with everyone here on earth, He is waiting.

Then, about as quickly as this love-filled energy that flowed from Him to me and back again came, it started to slowly leave. I was being carefully put back in my home here in this world. This exchange was filled with so much understanding, validation, and gratitude.

For me, God used this connection of unconditional love to grab me. I was changed forever that day, with a newly-defined purpose in life.

~ My purpose was to love, is to love.~

I've worked really hard at doing my best to share God's love. And, I have not been perfect! I mess up, but then quickly repent and naturally go back at it. So if my purpose was to simply love…I should feel at peace. Well, I did for years….and then something changed.

Something happened around two years ago. I started to feel bored or misdirected in my life. Then I began to feel unsettled, like God wanted me to do something. I recognized that I was being called to do more than where I was at currently. My editor asked me to elaborate here, so that those that might write this off as a midlife crisis, would be able to identify this as something different. I love and despise some of the areas I am having to adjust with edits.

The truth is, after I wrote this book and gave it to my editor, I knew it was good, but that it was not nearly good enough. I knew it needed work, but I didn't know how to make it better. I wrote the book without a lot of difficulty. I had so much of this book etched into my heart and into my life coaching work and business plans already. I knew God led me thus far and would carry me through, but I truly had no idea how to make the book better.

I gave the book to three wonderful people who are close to me, whom I value greatly and knew would speak the truth to me. They all said the same thing; add in more stories, carry my life coaching principles throughout the book, and work on flow.

So, in honoring my editor who found this place in the book in need of a story, I share the following.

Fifty is lurking around the corner. Two years ago our youngest daughter left for college and one might possibly wonder if I was going through a midlife crisis. I feel the same as I did five, ten, and twenty years ago. The only thing I can say that may shed a little light on this newly beginning transformation is that - this is how God works. We simply need to let him in. If He even enters through a little crack, He will grow in us, transform us and lead us.

This growing transformation in me, moved me to a place where I knew I could give and do more. Everyone's story is unique to them, and I absolutely love helping people get to a place where they are living out God's purpose for their life, living in the abundance Christ offers them, and abiding in their healthiest most fulfilled days. This is what I call the Living Legacy.

Another thing… **Who cares what folks think when we know we are doing good work and are on God's path!** (Okay, my editor was right, that felt GREAT!) But now, let's get back to the purpose at hand.

Until we get that unsettled feeling, like we are missing something, or not doing enough, we most likely ARE in our right place.

God will let you know when you are to step out, change, grow and/or be called to something else. Discontent grew loudly and stirred within me until I knew God wanted more from me.

Take a moment to consider just how God has and is working in you. Where has He, or may He, be 'CALLING' for your attention?

This is a little hard for me to share, but I want to be real, and I want to relate to anyone else finding themselves in a similar place. A place where they are doing fine…life is good, where they are doing good work and making a difference in other's lives, yet feeling that something is still missing. I have had such passion for my work as a nursing leader. I have had abundant energy to serve my patients, employees and peers. I truly love them and want the best for them.

One day it dawned on me that I was having to 'work' at giving to my job in the same ways that once filled me up. What I once did without thinking, and what once seemed a joyful challenge, I now did out of discipline; and it took more energy away from me than I was receiving. I felt bored at times and didn't know where this was coming from, because my care for all the work was still there. But the passion I once had was fading, and a new direction was being unveiled.

When I recognized this was happening, I prayed and made adjustments to stay engaged. I still have a couple of months left before my resignation is completed, and with great relief I can say I will make it and stay positively engaged until I leave my keys on my desk.

So maybe the key is recognizing your level of peace and passion in your place. While I definitely knew my purpose was changing, I did not, for one second, know how. I listened to my gut enough to know something was off. God was stirring in me, and He was going to give me the answers!

How you might ask? Do you ever ponder that very question? That would honestly be the Golden Ticket wouldn't it? To have direct access to God's absolute desires for your life!

I longed for words from my Father. I tried to repeat what I had done so many years ago as I held my sweet baby Raya, praying as earnestly as I could. But no profound connection came this time. The only thing I can say is I have learned over the years to trust my gut. I really shouldn't even call it that. The phrase should not be "Trust my gut" it should be "Trust my God." That is what I do, and that is what I did.

That flip, or sometimes pit in my stomach, I have learned to listen to. This is the Holy Spirit, and he should not be written off as an autonomic response to life. **Rather, the Holy Spirit is powerful enough to provide us with a physiologic response to heightened awareness.**

So, as I prayed and listened, repeated the prayer back differently and listened, prayed the next day and listened…doors would open and others would shut but I would just keep moving forward, one step at a time until I, without a doubt, knew I was on the right path, and then I followed.

As I became more convicted in this change, I remember a point where I was so invested in God and His plan for me, that I was actually nervous to pray. It scared me to know God might just tell me or ask me to do something I felt I was incapable of. And yet, I knew I would do it anyway. I kept asking and waiting.

Sometimes people think I just jumped in fearlessly and went for it; but I was afraid and completely secure at the same time. The afraid part came from two places that I will address in more detail later. Fear was trying to get the best of me. This fear was very worldly (insecurity-doubt), and it never spoke as loudly as the security and strength of knowing I was in God's hands.

For those of you who have a passion God has put in your heart but simply don't know how or where to begin, I want you all to know it was a process. I did it with one very calculated step at a time. I journaled through it all and turned this process into a usable tool. I use it now to coach clients struggling to find their God-given life purpose, for clarity, and action.

This process took me from nursing to coaching, coaching to speaking, and speaking to writing, because that is how the doors opened, and I learned to walk through them with God leading me. I was mindful to not push any doors open on my

> **Consider the Problem:** Are you listening to your heart, mind, and soul?
>
> It's easy to get off here. We need to go to God when we are in a place of uncertainty. We are prey when doubt of any kind is about.

own doing, and to not close any that I felt God had opened. I tested my options and watched God redirect me and correct my path-which I promptly followed while giving thanks to Him and His Glory.

If I had been asked to do everything I have done in the last nine months by any one person, I'd have said no way and laughed. But I was told in a loving whisper, by our Maker, to go and do, and I am.

God knew what I needed, and when I needed what, in order to proceed and grow. He was careful with me and I trusted him.

Here is my 12-month journey

While coaching and encouraging my clients to walk in faith, many will ask me how to trust. This is a personal thing, but I am learning that helping others see examples will give them some clarity, so here is the evidence I had of God's work which has kept me going. I hope it helps some of you.

In 2014 the healthcare organization I worked for was enforcing their directors to further their nursing degrees. I became a director of nursing for two nursing homes when I was twenty-six years old, and had been in healthcare leadership ever since. I really wasn't interested in going back to college at this point in my career. But as it was, if I was going back for my master's, I felt pulled to get it in counseling. I had picked my school, and planned to start in 2015. My youngest daughter, Riley, would be in college and it seemed like a nice time to go back. While doing research on the internet I must have been on some shared sites because counseling and coaching kept coming up together.

Door #1 LEAD
(not coincidence)

As I was studying online master's courses and programs, I clicked on one I really liked, but realized I was on a coaching site. I got off. The next morning, I woke up, grabbed my coffee, and got back on the computer. There it was again. LPI, Life

Purpose Institute. I realized how affordable it would be, how flexible it would be, how in line with my passion it was, and I decided there was no harm in trying.

Door #2 SUPPORT
(out of character, 'risky,' but showing great love)

Next, my husband. He is NOT a risk taker. But as I told him about the coaching he listened cautiously. Then he said, "I think you were made to do this." That was such a strange thing for him to say. Strange for him to consider me in a career he knew so little about. Strange for him to consider me leaving a pretty good and guaranteed salary. Strange for him not to buck the time or investment it would take, and strange for him to consider people are designed for specific work. (This was one of the most convincing parts of me giving it a try.)

Door #3 TIMING
(allowing a safety net which I felt I needed)

I got accepted into a class that would begin right after my daughter Raya's wedding, and would end right before college courses to get my master's would begin, if I felt I needed to do that after all.

Door #4 BIGGER
(bigger than what I'd dreamed for myself)

I learned that there was spiritual coaching in this institute, something that hadn't even crossed my mind. My intention this whole time was to jump in on the wave of healthcare changes coming down the pike. Changes that would require our hospitals, providers, and patients to be healthier and with less secondary effects of illnesses. While I chanced upon this coaching program, I did not investigate others, feeling so affirmed with this one. I had studied and studied which college to attend, not really sure which one to choose. Yet I knew right away which coaching program to use! As it turns out, my company's foundation today is faith based, and its success gained by keeping God at the foundation of it has been far more than I would have ever dreamed.

Door #5 ENERGY
(tapping into my driving force brought my passion back)

My passion was back! The classes were simple for me. Jeff was right, I was made for this and once again things that might have otherwise worn me out were filling me up. I built a website, ran an active blog, developed coaching programs, began doing events, coached many clients, obtained my certification, and began writing a book, which was all done while working fulltime.

I have to admit these extra work demands I knew were for a season, and I cannot wait to free up the hours of my current job to focus on God's work and the new clients I will serve when this time comes.

I love providing service through my company without restrictions of faith practices. Goal setting, leading, and inspiring has always been easy for me. Finding ways to get others to adopt ownership over their outcome and performance is very fulfilling. All through my work life I have loved watching my staff, coworkers and patients grow and learn...but now I am on my own.

With my private practice I quickly learned the most powerful way to ignite a soul to perform at it's highest level is to tap into it's driving force. Getting others back in line with their faith, for every aspect of their life, work, relationships, health.... THIS WAS GOOD! My clients were tapping into energy and growth they never knew they had....it was working and working well!!!!

Door #6 CONNECTIONS

God has been putting me in line with many people who have made such an impact on my business and growth. Many I have included in my book's acknowledgments. Here is a quick reference to some: One of my bosses supported me early on. I got into a Women's Expo in Des Moines after another vendor backed out at the last minute, Kary Oberbrunner has been the most amazing mentor in publishing this book and Godly business practices who I cannot say enough about, one of my dear friends has a marketing business and offers me countless advice, my pastor offered to review and comment on my book, my church reached out to offer scholarships to those who would like to coach with me but might need financial assistance, another influential pastor who helped my family learn to 'live' the Word offered a book endorsement, three people gave me honest book edits that I NEEDED, and I got an intern from our town's Christian college, Northwestern, in Orange City, Iowa, to offer help which timed perfectly for the launching of this book. (I am simply beside myself right now seeing this all on paper - such blessings.)

There were doors that shut before me too, and I told myself they must not have been part of God's plan; as I knew by then that I was working His plan for sure.

I share all this with you to encourage and inspire you as you begin to awaken to the legacy God has left behind specifically for you~

Let the redeemed of the Lord tell their story-
Psalm 107:2

THE WORD

CHAPTER 2

DO YOU WANT TO HEAR GOD SPEAK YOUR PURPOSE TO YOU?

I AM HIS AND HE IS MINE

I Am His & He Is Mine...

THE WORD

DO YOU WANT TO HEAR GOD SPEAK YOUR PURPOSE TO YOU?

Do you think I got my answer? Do you think it came in words? Sorry to say, no words. A big part of finding your God-given purpose is to know what God is asking of you.

Do you wish God would just tell you, in words, what to do... so you could hear it? Maybe write it all out for you?

I know I'm not the only one who just wishes God would speak audible words whenever we are lost or misdirected. Would you follow if He told you just what you are supposed to do? What if He wrote out exactly what your life purpose was? Would you read it and make work of it?

The Bible: God's living word written out for us...it tells us exactly what to do. How often do we use it?

In the beginning I was getting nudges, feelings, and intuition that led to doors opening but still wondered if they were simply coincidences. I even tried ignoring them in hopes that if they truly were God speaking to me, that He'd speak up!

Here is a personal story I reflected on that helped me to know just how to proceed in 'hearing God's requests of myself.' Through this story you will come to understand that we all have God's words to know our path.

My husband works for a grocery store chain that moved us around for years. I had the gift of working my early nursing years for a fabulous health system as a director of nursing. There I learned very strong leadership skills that I took with me everywhere we went.

Over the next several years we moved numerous times. I worked in places where there was no training, bad training, great training, and ridiculous training. But my core, from when I first learned to work in healthcare, was very strong. It always sustained me. It kept me thriving and my teams growing. You could plop me in any mess and my area would, person by person, unite, learn, and grow until we were proud of the work done today. Yet knowing we could do even better tomorrow.

The process I learned at such a beginning place in my career was **'good and right'**; and it carried me through all kinds of work environments and situations... helping me to always know how to respond.

~So as I questioned my next step, this had me thinking~

You could plop me in any mess and my area would, person by person, unite, learn, and grow until we were proud of the work done today. Yet knowing we could do even better tomorrow.

Maybe I needed to stop waiting for God to crack me with a bolt of lightening. Maybe I needed to go and get myself a true education, a strong foundation of God's **'good and right'** teachings. Maybe then I would know what God was asking of me and how to respond.

> **Consider the Problem:** The Bible...Look to 'The Word' to get your true and right foundation.
>
> **"A process, when true & right, will work anywhere, anytime."**

I come from a very small Christian community in Orange City, Iowa. I had spent the last several years of my adult life in Bible studies and attending church regularly, but I kept feeling like I needed to know more. Deciding to dive into the 'Word' at age 45 with newly found gusto wasn't so overwhelming for me here. I was in a wonderful church with two amazing pastors and many opportunities for learning.

But, what about people not in a welcoming Christian community?

This is when my true purpose started to take root. I was seeing how rapidly and successfully my coaching clients were transforming their lives when their faith was at the foundation of their growth and life. I was surprised it was not just myself that found the deepened level of faith, even at a mature age, to be so helpful. And I was on fire to share this with the world! On May 17, 2016, I added "Faith Infused Living ~ Reaching Goals Higher" to my marketing portfolio, and it speaks volumes to me and to the way I practice.

I was seeing many coaching clients who were raised in a Christian home but now, as an adult, this busy life was consuming their days, and they grew out of the routine of going to church, along with all it had to offer. Others had not grown up in a church community at all but definitely knew and loved their God.

These clients, when I mentioned getting into a routine of church and the 'Word,' like a Bible study or small group, would cringe or pull away in fear...doubt...insecurity of this unfamiliar request. Yet, they were more than accepting of adding in a few lifestyle changes that I recommended to help infuse faith back into their days, work, life and goals.

One of my most coached modules is on learning, and is titled the "Learning Legacy." Here I teach my clients how to use a wide range of tools to grow their lives through all God has to offer. Many of these tools are available to us all and we are using them everyday.

I simply share ways of using these to glorify God. Take the internet and our phones. They provide a vast array of ways to infuse faith into our days and fill our minds with sound answers, positive motivation, direction and guidance whenever we need it.

The internet, our computers, and our phones are poisonous tools to many; leading folks onto paths of destruction, misdirection and emptiness. But, it really is not the tool that gets us into trouble, it is the use of the tool. I love showing people all the gifts and the effectiveness these tools can provide when used for good.

This resistance of my clients to get involved or back into a church setting rarely came from lack of desire...but most always came back to lack of comfort and acceptance.

Really? Are 'WE' church goers turning people away by not welcoming and reassuring our neighbors of their acceptance in God's house? Do we not welcome our neighbors into our homes, our Bible studies, small groups, or into our Christian Lifestyle? I can't help but think of my own faith journey. What if I had not been welcomed in, how would I have grown? What about our sisters and brothers in Christ? How will they grow?

What about all of them...

*There is a gift for us **ALL**, it is **NOT** exclusive!*

"The BIBLE & the LIVING Word"

God's words are living and cannot only communicate what you are to do, these words can live in you and work in you, day after day, actually showing you how to live and grow. And, leading you to your God-given life purpose. We, as a nation, have gotten away from these living words.

It wasn't that long ago when most every home had a Bible, and often the family would read of it together. Unless you are blessed to still be carrying on with this tradition, most would find the thought of this unrealistic, outdated, and irrelevant in today's world.

> This is why I post free daily blogs sharing with the world how to apply the 'Word' into our daily lives.
> *nicciekliegl.com*

The world is using individual and worldly thoughts to decide what is good and right and true for not only themselves but for the rest of us. It isn't uncommon that I hear individuals tell me what is written in our Bible, and they are wrong! We need to know what is written and be comfortable enough to go and look when we wonder. It is in black and white, and with no need to feel threatened or defenseless we can stand up to what we know is the truth.

We can not get sucked into believing the world.

We do this by never leaving the 'Word'!

. . . and how from infancy you have known the Holy Scriptures, which are able to make you wise for salvation through faith in Christ Jesus. All Scripture is God-breathed and is useful for teaching, rebuking, correcting and training in righteousness, so that the servant of God[a] may be thoroughly equipped for every good work. 2 Timothy 3:15-17

So many of us are out and about, living by 'the body,' which too often brings self-destruction. This scares me. I want us to go to the one true light, true source of life, the Savior, the Almighty, the Omniscient (all-knowing), Omnipotent (all-powerful) and Omnipresent (always present) one. This is the process that works, that has worked for years, that will work forever...but only for those who so choose it.

God's Affirming Words on 'Life Purpose'

You are His & He is yours...

For he chose us in him before the creation of the world to be holy and blameless in his sight. In love he[a] predestined us for adoption to sonship through Jesus Christ, in accordance with his pleasure and will— Ephesians 1:4-5

- For those wanting to go deeper into their faith or find their faith for the first time, it's important to know that you do not need to be raised in any particular home, country, or status to be chosen, you already are adopted. You are already His...you simply need to believe it and let it set in and take root.

- "would be blameless" ... We were chosen **with** the understanding that we need to be **made** blameless. God knew and knows all of our sin, and he still chose us...we simply need to believe it and let it set in and take root.

- "through" Christ... according to Christ's kind intention. I love

> **Consider the Problem:** Could not truly loving ourselves affect how much we *allow* ourselves to be loved by God? Could how much love we accept by God affect how much we love others?
>
> This is why I made the 'Perfectly Imperfect' program, which is hugely successful with helping self-worth, self-love and self-esteem in a God-based way that I am so grateful for! (This is coming in Part 2)

that, not according to our works, our past, our family tree, or worldly position. According to Christ's kind intention…. let that set in and take root!

The Inheritance (a legacy left for us) …

In him we have obtained an inheritance, having been predestined according to the purpose of him who works all things according to the counsel of his will, Ephesians 1:11 ESV

- "inheritance" …why had these words never jumped out to me before. As I began coaching clients on finding their God given life purpose I kept coming across individuals that somehow felt unworthy for more. They were amazing individuals. I could see how much God loved them and I had to find a way to help them see what I could.
- THIS IS WHERE THINGS REALLY STARTED FOR ME! It starts with love. We all need to know just how loved by God we are before our first breath here even took place (predestined).

> **Consider the Problem:** God made us to do His will. So if we figure out just how we are uniquely designed, this will help tremendously in knowing our true calling.

- "according to His will" … Well this is the tricky part. For me, I think it comes down to trying to figure out His will for us by discovering how God specifically designed us.
- By keeping the focus on who God made us to be, I am seeing great success. I myself was racking my brains trying to figure out God's plan for me, when all I needed to do was really 'learn me' and how God made me. This was where I found my true calling. This is what I love

to help my clients do. This is much of the "I am His & He is Mine" program that I love so much!

Why fear? Because He has the power...

And we know that in all things God works for the good of those who love him, who have been called according to his purpose.. Romans 8:28

- I admit I was nervous to step out in faith and make work of working the plan I truly felt God designed for me, so I get how hard this can be. However, think on your fear. Is it fear of where He might take you-like it was for me? Or, is it fear of making a mistake, looking silly or flopping? One is worldly, one is Godly. One is wrong, and one is right.

- Either way, when stepping out IN FAITH, we can trust that God has got our back. He will be working things out for the good of us. Truly, what if you got it wrong and started out on a path that wasn't quite right....do you honestly think God is not capable of straightening your path and making it all work out somehow? You may find a whole new avenue laid before you.

- Romans 8:28 reminds us of God's support in our called purpose...for those who love Him.

> **Consider the Problem:** Do we trust Romans 8:28 and will we obey?
>
> I find myself humming these three small words regularly.
> *Trust and Obey*

Why?... For His purpose. NOT by works... by grace.

He has saved us and called us to a holy life—not because of anything we have done but because of his own purpose and grace. This grace was given us in Christ Jesus before the beginning of time, 2 Timothy 1:9

- "called by GRACE" ...the thing that sets Christians apart in faith is NOT that we are better than any other God loving individual. It is our belief that by the grace of God we are assured of our eternal life from the point of understanding what Jesus did for us...no act can assure us of this gift prior to our bodily death.

- Receiving this gift comes with responsibility, and until you have experienced it, one cannot understand how this responsibility is partnered with the acceptance. It's a response to this great gift... NOT like a direct deposit payment on a rent to own possession. This gift is paid in full.

- Many search for their life purpose because they feel this desire to do more, an accountability to self and God to do as much as they possibly can. I believe we simply know we function really well when we are in a good place.

Why is it so important, to know my gift?...

Now there are varieties of gifts, but the same Spirit; and there are varieties of service, but the same Lord; and there are varieties of activities, but it is the same God who empowers them all in everyone. To each is given the manifestation of the Spirit for the common good. 1 Corinthians 12:4-7

- One gift is no better than the next. They become awesome with our action. First, we need to truly know our gift and then we need to act on it. What good is faith without action. What good is talent never developed?

- Churches often do gift tests and I love this...but sometimes it is done with the wrong heart. Gift tests are valuable and I put a lot of effort into teaching people how to use their gifts wisely. It's not enough to simply know a gift you carry, it's just as important to know how to use it. (This is expounded on in the Sweet Spot Study I coach on…pieces of this I will go over in chapter four.)

Just looking at these few verses shows such insight to gaining understanding of our calling and our acceptance to all the gifts God wants to give us. The 'Word' has so much to offer us, in all areas of our life. We simply need to use it.

Here are a few steps I like to share with new users of the Bible. As you read this book, whether you are alone or doing this in a Bible study or group….one of the most important things I want to stress is 'any level of faith.' Again, we are all in different places, and we are here to help each other grow and share God's word.

One of the most awesome things about God's Word is gaining new insight as the years pass. What you once didn't understand later makes complete sense. For some of you these tips are not new and you may have more to share with new comers-so please do. And while reading the Bible, when you read things that increased your wisdom- share that too.

5 Steps for Insight when turning to the WORD

1. **Pray first:** For guidance and to be able to accept what is written, and to be able to apply His will to your life.
2. **Deliberating over a concept is okay:** If something does not make sense, reread the paragraph or chapter again. If you still do not understand, write down the problem area and continue onward. You may discover the answers later in your reading. (I truly believe God shows you meaning as you are able and ready to absorb.)
3. **Journaling or taking notes is a great idea:** This way you can see your insight increase with time and gained knowledge. Some buy a cheap Bible and write notes all over it.
4. **Interpretive Footnotes:** It's so helpful to look at the notes included in your Bible. Get a teaching Bible if you really want some interpretation.

5. **One bite at a time:** The Word will sustain you. Do not try and devour it all at once or you may lose insight.

6. **Start with the New Testament:** We need to follow God's will for us today, not just the Old Testament which was intended for the Jews according to the law. The New Testament Gospel is what structures our understanding as Christians today. Then you can look to the Old Testament later with new understanding and insight that really makes those verses speak clarity. However, I have to say Proverbs is also a great way to start a habit of reading the "Word" ....with 31 chapters, providing one chapter per day in a given month for reading.

THE GIFT

CHAPTER 3

DO YOU KNOW WHAT YOUR LIFE PURPOSE WILL GIVE YOU OR WHAT NOT KNOWING MAY TAKE?

I AM HIS AND HE IS MINE

I Am His & He Is Mine...

THE GIFT

DO YOU KNOW WHAT YOUR LIFE PURPOSE MAY GIVE YOU OR WHAT NOT KNOWING MAY TAKE?

Hindsight is 20/20 indeed. When considering the outcome of living out the purpose God has intended for you, wouldn't it be grand to really know what your life would look like in accordance to acting on God's gift or not? I do hope you come to enjoy the "Consider the Gift" chapters within each part of this book. This chapter offers hope, especially knowing that He can provide far more than we could ever dream.

"Now glory be to God, by his mighty power at work within us is able to do far more than we would ever dare to ask or even dream of — infinitely beyond our highest prayers, desires, thoughts, or hopes." Ephesians 3:20 Living Bible (TLB)

I cannot help but think of the game show, "Let's Make a Deal." Oh, how the contestants labored over which curtain to look behind, to discover what prize they would end with. It wouldn't have even been a show if the curtains were open for all the world to see, and the options were laid out right before them. Surely each contestant would have no trouble picking the most valuable gift.

Here we will pull back the curtains on our faith, to find the truth and to see just what we are saying yes to, and what we are passing by.

For I know the plans I have for you," declares the Lord, "plans to prosper you and not to harm you, plans to give you hope and a future. Jeremiah 29:11

Is it just that we don't let ourselves believe in this prosperous future? Or do we think we are unworthy? Does it feel like we are using God?

When it comes to faith, we sometimes pick and choose which verses to believe. The truth is we either believe or we don't. So maybe what we are doing is deciding which verses to **live by.**

Does this sort of make you cringe or sound familiar? The Word, our navigational direction for 'good' living, folded up and tucked away...away from our hearts, minds, and souls. We need to learn to accept Jeremiah 29:11 just as we do the other verses in the Bible. This verse clearly affirms to us that God's plan is to give us prosperity, hope and a future.

Consider the Gift: We can live by all, some, or none of the Word... and therefore receiving all, some or none of it's wisdom, support and guidance. It's our choice.

Maybe it has more to do with us wondering what God's definition of prosperity is.

We sure can't complain about receiving hope and a future. So then, is it fear that keeps us from pulling open the curtain to our God-appointed gifts and prosperity?

So many of us accept the challenge of investing in our future on our own merit, yet hesitate to move from the driver's seat to the passenger's seat when venturing out on God's path.

Think about it. Most of us study, prepare, and seek out resources that will teach us skills and result in jobs. We often invest thousands of dollars and years of schooling. We push on through our training, hoping to acquire the worldly results of this work and to land a lucrative career. We don't exactly know what the job will be in the end, but we go about putting our trust in the system, in our studies, and we step out in faith. But faith of whom? Of ourselves... of our hard work... of the world?

> **Consider the Gift:** With your free will here on earth, do you choose God as your pilot who knows every path, and who has all the required knowledge and strength to get you there? Or will all your hope be based off your own merit?

Why do you suppose we often believe in our own power, strength, and work over God's?

We are human and wonderful creatures, but don't we want the supernatural if we can have it? Don't we want all the insight, strength, and compassion God can offer?

Remember the verse on spiritual gifts in 1 Corinthians 12:4-7: *God who empowers them all in everyone. To each is given the manifestation of the Spirit.*

God is empowering us with our gifts and the Holy Spirit helps us work these gifts. What better mentor can we have?

> **Consider the Gift:** The Holy Spirit as our mentor. God as our recruiter....
>
> How could we not land a better career path or life path with these two at our side?

41

I would love nothing more than for us all to know what our God-given gifts are, what our worldly skills are, and to find a place where we use them to serve each other, in the most powerful way possible. This is a beautiful place.

A place where God, the world, and we 'join-up'!

I use this term 'join-up' for a reason. It takes trust and patience. It involves a master, an environment and a follower for true joining up.

The term 'join-up' comes from a man named Monty Roberts, the founder of this horse training term. (www.montyroberts.com/ab_about_monty/ju_about) He reports that 'Join-Up' methods rely on horse and trainer establishing a bond of communication and trust. *"You must somehow understand that we as horsemen can do very little to teach the horse. What we can do is to create an environment in which he can learn." Monty says, "We hear that 'actions speak louder than words,"* …

When I am life coaching I do not want my clients to need me or depend on me. I teach faith-infused growth and living, because there is so much value from living within a Christian environment and depending on God.
Once we get accustomed to the tools and resources, they will ignite a lifetime of action from our Almighty.
I have a passion for inspiring others to gain all they can by joining up with God. The 'Word' is their syllabus, the Holy Spirit their guide, and Jesus Christ their Savior. Once they learn to depend and trust in this unbreakable bond, I can hardly hold myself down with joy and gratitude. At this time, they start their journey in the *Living Legacy*.
I am amazed and proud of individuals who trust in themselves, in their work, and who understand that there most often is payoff for hard work. However, all this is a discussion

of 'worldly' cause and effect, which we will get into more later. I see individuals satisfied with hard work and its effects, and they stop there, being content with themselves and their world. However, when individuals combine their hard work in this world with the power of God, great things happen. **When we combine all our good work with God's work...there is no stopping us!**

What I so passionately want to see is everyone finding their sweet spot. The place where an individual's worldly skills align with their heavenly talents and gifts, where they can embrace the life God has designed for them to live in, work in, grow in, and give in.

An example of greatness that comes out of someone's worldly work and God-given talent joining up is Julia Child's story. Julia received a good education, was from a prominent family, stood six foot two, and excelled in women's sports. She used this education (worldly skill), was respected by the CIA, and performed well in WWII as head of the Registry of the OSS Secretariat. When Julia was asked to help solve the problem of too many OSS underwater explosives being set off by curious sharks...she honorably and successfully concocted a recipe known as shark repellent to ward off the sharks, which is still used today. She most definitely received positive effects and success of her skillful hard work. She also used her spiritual gift of cooking to make this happen.

I believe Julia found her calling in the culinary arts and not in her very noble service to her country. Recorded in history, in an interview with *The New York Times*, Julia reported her travels and French dining, exposing her to *"an opening up of the soul and spirit for me."* She went on to gain far more than anything she imagined, when she returned from the service and began her true passion and worked her gifts.

There are different kinds of gifts, but the same Spirit distributes them. 1 Corinthians 12: 4

> **Consider the gift:** A measure of faith that equals the Spirit.

Could your true purpose be held captive by what you allow yourself to believe?

As we develop sound plans for our future, and carry them out with execution, we can most definitely do good work and live a very successful and content life. Those that make their life's work be one of noble, praiseworthy, excellent design, will not only receive success of their calculated, well-executed actions, but will also receive the Godly fruits of those labors.

You will eat the fruit of your labor; blessings and prosperity will be yours. Psalm 128:2

However, I believe when one's life purpose is nowhere to be found, it simply remains stage fright behind the curtains of faith. When the curtains of faith are flung open, in comes light that will reach your soul, insight that will guide you with clarity and truth, and a warmth that will reach out to touch all those in your presence. This is the life purpose I want to see take hold of each and every soul that walks this earth.

A perfect example is John, a single dad raising two girls. His wife left him and the girls when they were ten and twelve. His mother is no longer alive and he is an only child. He is a recruiter and has flexible hours. He is quite good at his job but admits he does well at work to keep his job and to be respected, but he is not very passionate about his work-life.

He seeks coaching for feeling ill-equipped to care for two young girls, one approaching her teens fast. He feels overwhelmed and is having a hard time keeping everything afloat.

End result: His gifts and talents show him to be gifted in craftsmanship and discernment. He started a Bible Study with the girls that they'd picked out online together and does it every night before bed. This has helped bring the girls closer to him again, and has taken off much of the pressure and stress he was feeling.

He recognized lack of community and support could be remedied by getting involved in a church community and one has welcomed them in warmly, which has changed their lives. He is using his gifts and talents of craftsmanship, as well as his worldly skill as a recruiter to build an exchange skills program within his church. Within this program, members of the congregation who have needs are partnered with those who have the desired skills.

He also has a network of church connections now, whom he trusts to help him with the girls, and he helps other members where he has much to offer. John is in a great place…In the Living Legacy Program I call this the sweet spot.

Right about now I wonder if you might be questioning just where you are, in living out the legacy Jesus has left behind for you. When we have thoughts of self evaluation, that is great- but do not let them shift to doubt. It is good to evaluate and call on God for answers! Let's not look to the world for our reassurance to life performance.

I absolutely love it when my clients land in the place where they have healed from many of the roadblocks and hurdles they have been working on, and then find themselves ready to get busy living.

This is a small but powerful self-evaluating tool which is built into one of my 'Learning Legacy' coaching programs on finding your God-given life purpose. (It's a great mental check designed to help spur you to move forward in life with the plan God has designed specifically for YOU.)

God-given Life Purpose…God's WORK designed for you!

W…Willed by God? Here we use several checks and tools to evaluate different life paths. We do not move forward until we know the one to test is in line with our Maker.

O...Open to evangelize? No worries, I do not mean you need to hit the streets with your Bible in hand. And at the same time...that is what I am talking about. Here we look at how our life purpose is a witness to others. Does it allow us to be examples of Christ? Are we making believers of others simply by the work we do, and how we do it?

R...Responsive? How responsive are we? As you continue reading *Awaken the Living Legacy* you will see a very accountable response to Jesus's gift of Grace. How service minded is our plan? How responsive to God and others is our life purpose? Does it include loving our neighbor...serving?

K...Keeping in faith. Does the plan for your life purpose include measures to keep you deeply rooted in your faith? We can actually dismantle a beautiful plan God has written in our heart by getting caught up 'in the world.' You are either in or out. We cannot serve two Gods (It's God or the World) I put a lot of energy and passion into helping others root deeply into their faith...where they no longer fall prey to the world.

Consider the gift: The Living Legacy

I want you to find your sweet spot; where your passion comes from a faith that dwells deep within your soul. Where you move forward in your plans, growth and goals with ease and clarity. Where you carry with you a level of energy that others feel, desire to have, and spreads throughout our nation.

THE CHOICE

CHAPTER 4

DO YOU KNOW YOU'VE MADE YOUR CHOICE ON WORKING YOUR LIFE PURPOSE ALREADY?

YOU ARE HIS AND HE IS YOURS

I Am His & He Is Mine...

THE CHOICE

DO YOU KNOW YOU'VE MADE YOUR CHOICE ON LIVING YOUR LIFE PURPOSE ALREADY?

"The earth is crying for people who make sound judgment and informed decisions." -Sunday Adelaja

Do you know that you may have made your choice on living your life purpose already? While coaching, I have come to understand this more than I would have ever dreamed. People refrain from moving forward with a decision for all kinds of reasons. I hope you find yourself challenged by each of the 'Consider the Choice' chapters found within each part of this book.

The thing is, making no decision, whatever the reason, is a decision... It's a "no"!

Something even more significant is that deciding to move forward in faith, is a "yes"! Regardless of how you move forward, whether it be rough or smooth terrain, it remains a "yes"!

"Whoever can be trusted with very little can also be trusted with much, and whoever is dishonest with very little will also be dishonest with much." Luke 16:10

What about our faith? Isn't faith a yes or no? Don't we either believe or not? I fear sometimes people write themselves off when hoping for more, looking to the right or left and seeing another who seems deeper or more committed in their faith or their journey. This is not how God works.

When one accepts Christ, they're in, period. They are living and breathing children of God who are our sisters and brothers in Christ.

As we allow ourselves to go deeper (meaning anything from giving yourself to Christ, to simply infusing faith into your walk), so will our measure of faith. However, you are still with Christ regardless of the place. Just keep thinking forward, moving forward, gaining more, and deepening your faith.

Never consider someone else's faith journey better or worse than your own; you are simply at a different place –NOT A BETTER ONE!

Faith is faith to God. Of course we want to grow in our faith, and we will feel the fruits of that blessing as well. Just focus on growing. In future chapters we will dive deeply into how to do this, until then just stay in the 'Word,' however it works best for you; blogs, daily Bible readings, music, podcast and more. Get yourself around believers (look to the church) that will offer you sound advice and be an example of Godliness to you, and pray frequently for everything in faith.

"For by the grace given me I say to every one of you: Do not think of yourself more highly than you ought, but rather

think of yourself with sober judgment, in accordance with the faith God has distributed to each of you." Romans 12:3

I like this verse because it reminds us that there is always something higher than oneself. I am who I am as a result of God, just as the next is. I like to think of this verse as an attitude adjustment…but we cannot leave off the element of faith discussed. Faith grows just like love. As we love more, so does our love for God. As we trust God more, so grows our faith. It goes hand and hand. If we trust God on our path He will grace us with fruits of the labor worked there.

So now I see faith as a gift and a choice. We choose faith, and want loads of it. We need to be wise with the level of faith gained. This discipline will bear fruit and will increase according to God in which we might bear more again. And this cycle will continue and will grow.

> **Consider the Choice:** Transformation… It's one thing to choose to believe. However, it is life transforming to **live by your faith.**

As we stay in the 'Word' and on God's path, our faith grows and so will our distribution of faith from God. It is a beautiful circle. God does not pick and choose His gifted few. He has made us ALL gifted and talented.

Let's work on staying in the 'Word,' growing our faith, increasing our measure, and increasing our effect on this world, in God's name.

One of the most wonderful parts about owning 'God's place'

> **Consider the Choice:** Do you have conviction to first know your gifts and talents, and more importantly, dare to use them?

in our talent and success, is that it means every possible ground for boasting is taken away. How can we boast if the qualification for receiving our gifts is never ours to begin with? Our good work comes from acting on our gifts given to us by God, and using them wisely. Our credit comes from working our talent, but it all starts and ends with the Glory to God.

I want nothing more than to help others to come to this place. The place where they are seeking God first to ensure they are living in their right place, feeling empowered by carrying out their life in what I call their sweet spot.

> "*Your* sweet spot; *the place where you are not swayed by outside influences, where you are strong and fulfilled, living at peace and confident about your purpose and life direction.*"

The S.W.E.E.T. SPOT Experiment

S=Study yourself…
- What type of activities or settings do you find yourself with loads of energy?
- What situations do you respond to very well?
- What things make you feel happy or leave you smiling or content?
- *What gets you upset, or frustrated easily?*
- *What sucks the life out of you?*

W=Welcome input…
- What thing(s) do others compliment you on?
- What do others turn to you for help with?

E=Examine what you admire in others…
- List traits or skills that you admire in others.
- List names of individuals you have a lot of respect for.
- List types of training or learned skills you enjoy acquiring.

E=Extract this information out in writing…
- Take a sheet of paper, draw a line straight down the center of the paper.

- On the RIGHT side put down all the items you learned from S=Studying yourself and from what you learned from W=Welcoming input (DO NOT use the underlined portion at this point)
- On the LEFT side write down the items you gathered by the E=Examining others portion.

T=Turn to the 'Word'...
- Use your findings to begin searching in the 'Word.'

This experiment works great because it forces us to use both sides of our brain. Why do you suppose the Bible so often pairs the heart, mind, and soul together...this is complete. We don't always allow our emotions to play with facts. (I have a wonderful coaching program, *'Emotional Intelligence,'* that goes deeper on this subject and teaches my clients how to use both in a way that compliments each other, and works most successfully.)

➡ **This is where our world keeps getting us into trouble. A single emotion is NOT an all-encompassing truth.**
- I feel like a girl so I am a girl
- I feel good when I do this so this is good

➡ **We also cannot expect what we KNOW is the truth to reach the world without a heart and soul to live it.**
- **This is our job. God appointed us to this job...**

"And this gospel of the kingdom will be preached in all the world as a witness to all the nations, and then the end will come." Matthew 24:14

Regardless of how right or left brained we are, ALL of us need to learn how to call on each side when needed.

Consider the Choice: Using both emotionally committing AND intellectually engaging... (The right and left side of your brain).

This provides you the with gain, growth and connection. What happens is the intellectual steps one needs to take while planning and carrying out a goal are engaged through the heart and soul.

Out of discipline anyone can perform detailed steps for a season, but with time they most often grow weary. When the intellectual plan is partnered with their emotions, there is great passion involved and this is the difference between someone doing good versus exceptional!

Real Spiritual/Life Coaching Example

On the right side of this client's Sweet Spot she wrote that she gained energy and felt alive when she was creating or designing things. On the left she wrote down that she admired Joanna Gains and how she turns a blank clean slate into a warm and welcoming home. She also wrote down that others would tell her she was good at preparing for events like hosting others into her home and helping at school or church functions.

This woman had been an awesome 'at home mom' and now was an empty nester. She felt bored and unfulfilled. She desperately wanted to offer something to society and to do her part, but simply wasn't sure what her part was.

With a lot of self-evaluating, turning to God, and discovering blind faith, she found her sweet spot...

She now works at a nearby shelter. She prepares rooms for the incoming tenants. She takes great pride in welcoming in new women and families. She was asked to freshen up the newcomer's room. She turned this love into a much more successful venture with a team of volunteers by redesigning the rooms with class and comfort, gathering donated items for décor, serving at a welcome gathering for all the new tenants, and offering an ongoing connection to these individuals through service and prayer.

She has found her sweet spot, and God is sweetening up her life and the lives around her. She is using her God-given talent 'service,' her worldly skill 'home-making,' and her love and passion for design and creating a warm comfort in the place one calls home. She is abiding in the Living Legacy!

LIFE PURPOSE
YOUR WINNING COMBINATION

1. Now that you have your two sides filled in, draw lines between items that match up. Living in a place where you are spiritually (emotionally) being filled and analytically (logically) skilled at is ideal.

2. Before we get to T=Turn to the 'Word,' I encourage you to take a Gifts and Talents assessment. There are many tools out there, and here is a link to my website which contains my favorite and the one I use, but it is just one of many examples. nikkiekliegl.com

3. Now take your Gifts and Talents findings and mark any common items from it that match your findings from your Sweet Spot experiment.

Your winning combination can be found
but it is your choice to work it!

PART 2
PERFECTLY
IMPERFECT

THE PROBLEM

CHAPTER 5

ARE YOU LOOKING THROUGH GODLY EYES OR WORLDLY EYES?

PERFECTLY IMPERFECT

PERFECTLY IMPERFECT

THE PROBLEM

ARE YOU LOOKING THROUGH GODLY EYES OR WORLDLY EYES?

The next four chapters (Part 2) of this book touch on one of my favorite coaching programs, "Perfectly Imperfect." Here we will repeat our format providing four chapters of clarity on this subject. 'Consider the Problem' is our focus in chapter five-and so it begins.

The world is harsh. The world teaches us to be harsh. To judge, to rate, to measure, to compare. The world also teaches us that this costly world value then determines our self-worth. Thankfully we don't all buy into it. And more importantly, it is very far from the truth. I have coached clients who questioned their value over many different worldly views. I am passionate about dispelling their validity with the truth... our seniors have much to offer, and our looks have nothing to do with our joy, love or success. Our children are wise far beyond our understanding. Our size is a number that measures the physical, not the heart, mind or soul. Mental illness is not of the weak, rather the strong beyond belief. I could go on and on.

In this chapter we will consider the eyes we view ourselves with as well as the eyes we view others with. We will dispel all notion of our self-worth matching up with worldly successes or failures. This chapter will show you how through Christ there is so much glory tucked within your imperfections. This will lead you to a place where you are most capable of growth and increase.

I keep asking that the God of our Lord Jesus Christ, the glorious Father, may give you the Spirit[a] of wisdom and revelation, so that you may know him better. I pray that the eyes of your heart may be enlightened in order that you may know the hope to which he has called you, the riches of his glorious inheritance in his holy people, Ephesians 1:17-18

● ● ●

I was around ten years old and sitting in reading class. The bell had just rung, and I was preparing for this difficult task of trying to read. I prayed that it wouldn't be an out loud reading day and focused on trying to sound out anything I could before I might get called upon. Instead, there was an announcement over the PA and several names were listed off for all the school to hear...mine being one of them. They asked us to meet in some room that I was unfamiliar with.

At first, I was relieved to be saved by the bell, and then dread set in as I knew something was wrong.

As we each filed out of our respective classrooms, I noticed in the hallway one other boy who seemed to be wearing the same cautious expression I was. I rather clung to this boy, and he to me as we were crammed into a very inappropriately small room for us.

I listened to the teacher explain that we were in there to get extra help with reading. I believed her. It seemed she genuinely wanted to help us. Some kids laughed and joked, making fun of themselves even, and I hated that. I simply did what I could to keep from tearing up at this chance to learn to read. 'Wouldn't that be great if I would be able to read?'

With a hopeful heart, I decided right then and there that I would do whatever they said and I would leave here a reader.

We spent the next weeks "reading." Actually, we spent the next few weeks memorizing our own very simple book. I went from totally committed and hopeful to disillusioned and upset. Some kids had trouble memorizing on top of everything else, and I remember feeling so badly for them.

> **Consider the Problem:** So much of our success lies in our hope.
>
> *"If for no other reason, this is why I was in this class. To understand that I had nothing to complain about, at least I could memorize."*

One day the teacher said we would have a gathering with our parents for them to see all we'd learned. I was so confused. Did they think we didn't all know we couldn't read…that we learned nothing?

Then they had us get up one evening in front of all our parents and 'read' our book to the whole group. My mom was smiling so broadly. She was amazed and a part of me wanted to pretend I could read. But the clear-headed part of me knew the truth.

> **Consider the problem:** Are we owning the truth of our weaknesses? (Are we being transparent with ourself and God which is needed to grow).

If we don't admit our weakness, how can we give it to God or ask for His help? We wouldn't then think we need help.

I was still a child then. God's child, and the world had not yet gotten its clenches on me. My mother gave me an immense amount of unconditional love, and I had no understanding of value being attached to performance yet.

Having the faith, joy, and hope that a child often does, made all the difference for me. I had no idea, at that time, how helpful this untainted hope and faith would be.

Looking back, I sometimes think how different life would have been had I tried to put up a front or even believed that I *should* be more. There were so many good things that resulted when I 'owned up,' that I would have been robbed the benefit of, had I pretended or covered up my weakness.

Because of this reading problem, I became more assured of my intelligence in other areas. I learned to adapt and got really good at listening. I am good at copying something and repeating it back. And, something I am so grateful for, is a rapid and detailed ability to problem solve.

The boy I met in our special ed class became my friend, and we spent every recess reading for the whole year.

I knew I needed to work harder if I wanted to **do more**. But, I never felt my person needed to **be more**.

Consider the problem: How do we let our imperfections AFFECT us, good and bad?

Hope and Determined or Shame and Despair.

---

*It's okay to let our imperfections **affect us**...*
*but it is not okay to let them **become us**.*

While understanding that loving yourself, just as you are and having faith in God's promise to bring good out of bad is a key part of this perfectly imperfect concept...

There is one way to check on your level of ownership to this belief of being perfectly imperfect! I use a process for checking this, called **"Inside-out."** I use it all the time to help people gain insight to just how deeply seeded a belief is in their heart, mind, and soul.

Sometimes people love others but not themselves, causing dependence or self-destruction. Sometimes people will take care of others but not themselves, setting themselves up for burnout. When you really own a belief, you live and breathe it.

To live it means it is a part of YOU.

To breathe it means you give it out to the WORLD.

So when you truly see yourself as perfectly imperfect- you will not only have grace and hope in your own place, you will also begin to see others and treat others with this same level of grace and encouragement for the place they are at!

How do you see others?

A psychologist who lectured my nursing class before doing our psych rotation shared this story that I will never forget.

Two nursing students had spent most of his early lecture being loud and disruptive, making fun of the situations he had been explaining. I do believe he graciously saw this behavior as a response to their nerves or comfort level. Regardless, he decided to break off from his lecture to share this story with us. He went on to ask us to each think about our life.

● ● ●

Now, imagine two lives each being lived out in a massive clear glass. Inside one glass is a man whose life has not gone so well. He has no job, his clothes are dirty, his body not clean. He doesn't have a home and has a horrible time keeping relationships going. He has lost contact with his wife and children, which brings him great despair.

Now, in another glass you see a different man. He is wearing a suit and is walking into a lovely home after a hard day's work at a very successful business. His wife and children greet him at the door and his long day melts away. He quietly sends a prayer off to his Father for such rich blessings and begins his evening at home.

Now, let's consider that as God chose the perfect spirit for the 'blessed' man's life, he chose you. He knit you into this blessed place, just so. God knew the path you would take and knew your trials and blessings before the first beat of your heart. God knew the sins of your forefathers and theirs before them... knowing you would be the perfect soul for this man's life.

Nice, huh? Makes you smile and be grateful for what you have doesn't it?

But wait, what about the soul who took on the other life?

Again, God knew the trials this life would bear, knew the sins of that man's forefathers and his before him. Wouldn't God then choose a measurable soul? So, would it be weak and unworthy? God knew the strength this soul would need to bear while carrying this load. God knew He needed to choose a great, mighty, forgiving and humble soul to take seat in that life.

A great, mighty, forgiving and humble soul to take seat in that life? What? Wait, that changes things! What if we who seem so blessed, are not the deeply strong, capable, faithful and gracious spirits we so appropriately deem ourselves?

He stared at us with eyes that pierced my soul and said, "You have no idea what these people have been up against. Their glass has been smeared with sins they didn't do, mental illness that arrived for reasons they do not know, disabilities that put them at a disadvantage, homes that did not build them up but tore down." He said, "Most of you are looking through some pretty clean glasses, and I wonder just how well you would do stuck living your life in their smeared up world. A world that when you try looking out at, through the mess of your hardships, looks completely different, void of beauty."

He told us that it was our job to look at the hearts of our patients and not their life.

66

> **Consider the problem:** It's our sinful nature to use worldly eyes and it takes a partnership with God to use Godly eyes.

'Give me your eyes Lord.'

I still weep when I share this story. It changed my life and how I view others forever.

Seeing yourself through Godly eyes requires faith, knowing that God will do as He promises and He will bring good out of the bad for no other reason than because HE LOVES US THAT MUCH...that is the only reason.

Seeing others through Godly eyes will allow you to recognize their strength and all their greatness, where by grace you will see the potential that can result from their trials. This will often spur you to do God's work and to help your neighbor that God plants before you.

If we see people through God's eyes, we see their heart, recognize them as our neighbor, or sister or brother, and we will do as Jesus would and as God desires of us.

Loving yourself is so important in being able to love others. God's love starts it all. The first four chapters of this book focus on learning that God's desire for our life stems from no other reason than love. In these four chapters of Perfectly Imperfect, we focus on learning to use God's love to love ourselves and others.

"Teacher, which is the greatest commandment in the Law?" Jesus replied: "'Love the Lord your God with all your heart and with all your soul and with all your mind.' This is the first and greatest commandment. And the second is like it: 'Love your neighbor as yourself.' All the Law and the Prophets hang on these two commandments." Matthew 22:36-40

THE WORD

CHAPTER 6

ARE YOU AWARE OF GOD'S CRAFTSMANSHIP?

PERFECTLY IMPERFECT

PERFECTLY IMPERFECT

THE WORD

ARE YOU AWARE OF GOD'S CRAFTSMANSHIP?

We are in the 'Consider the Word' Chapter of part two on Perfectly Imperfect, and I feel there is no verse that captures this understanding better than Psalms 139:13-16… **where the truth of your perfection comes to life!**

> *For you created my inmost being; you knit me together in my mother's womb. I praise you because I am fearfully and wonderfully made; your works are wonderful, I know that full well. My frame was not hidden from you when I was made in the secret place, when I was woven together in the depths of the earth. Your eyes saw my unformed body; all the days ordained for me were written in your book before one of them came to be.* Psalm 139:13-16

Coaching people of all sizes, shapes, ages and for so many different reasons, I find myself constantly impressed and surprised.

I am impressed on just how perfectly beautiful they are to begin with.

There is something so wonderfully beautiful about people being:

1. Trusting enough to open up.
2. Daring enough to want to grow.
3. Humble enough to admit weaknesses in need of change.

Then, I find myself in awe of their transformation, growth, and life in a new place; still as perfect as before, but now showing even more beauty and grace.

Why do we doubt our perfection when our imperfection can be used to perfect us?

> **Consider the word:** Too often we seek worldly measures to fix our imperfections. The world is flawed, so why do we do this?
>
> The world can just give us more of the same, but Christ...
>
> *For the sake of Christ, then, I am content with weaknesses, insults, hardships, persecutions, and calamities. For when I am weak, then I am strong. 2 Corinthians 12:10*

The 'Word' is the heart behind this tool which I use when coaching people on self-worth and the Perfectly Imperfect Program. The devil will use whatever he can to get a grip on you, and he loves to pounce when we are weak or down on ourselves. God knows that using our imperfections as a way to build us up, if we so choose, will not only teach us, but it will also give us a deeper appreciation for our blessings.

This tool is designed to remind us that...

It is not our imperfections that makes us less, it is how we let our imperfections have an E.F.F.E.C.T. on us that robs us of being more.

72

The Perfect E.F.F.E.C.T.

E= EVALUATE: How did you get here? I have found that there are often 3 situations that land someone in a place where self-worth, self-esteem, or self-love are lacking.

- A Major Life Incident; maybe a divorce that completely turned someone's world upside down, a death in the family or even the loss of a job and/or big financial loss.
- Outside Circumstances; this may be with an individual that was raised in a very critical home, maybe emotionally abused, bullied, etc.
- Worldly Standards become our reality; this happens easily. Outside influences are pouring into our ears and flashing before our eyes at an alarming rate. It happens on almost every television station, even the news. The lyrics to songs are becoming so destructive to one's self worth, that my stations have now narrowed to two or three versus the turn dial I once used without caution. We simply cannot let these falsehoods be our measure of self-worth.

All three adoptions of falsehood can be remedied! God, who is righteous, has made you in a way that will allow these imperfections to be part of your healing, growth, and blessings... and ultimately a part of His glory.

I simply love how doing my initial assessment with people can be so healing. Notice how this section speaks of falsehoods? When a client and I go over their assessment we begin to reveal many of the falsehoods they have come to believe. Simply being open to the truth takes away all the power of lies, and the transformation begins that simply.

F= FIND truth: Reread Psalms 139: 13-16 again. There are two truths that I want you to sit on. First, that God knit you together with nothing hidden. He knows exactly WHAT-you-are and WHO-you-are, and the Almighty craftsman did it anyway because to Him this is part of your perfection. Much of who you are is also because of your heritage. He has that covered too. He knows the sins of your father, and your father's father that were born unto you. This too He knows, and it is still part of your perfect design.

Second, "It sits right in your soul." Many of us can own the idea that God knows us completely, but then we still need to step out in faith and trust that who we are is enough. That sounds odd doesn't it? That something God made, might not be made very well. Who are we kidding? God knows what He is doing, and He knew YOU when He made You...just as you are!

Are you starting to buy into the idea that you are who you were designed to be?

- *But then what if you want to be more?*
- *Ah ha, I love that! Yes, what if you want to be more?*

F= FEELING: like you want to be more... One might wonder then, if that is NOT accepting yourself as you are today. I hear this ALL the time. And NO! This is growth, this is healthy, and this is what God wants for you.

> *Do not conform to the pattern of this world, but be transformed by the renewing of your mind. Then you will be able to test and approve what God's will is--his good, pleasing and perfect will.* Romans 12:2

So, how do we go about acquiring God's will for our life?

> *And without faith it is impossible to please God, because anyone who comes to him must believe that he exists and that he rewards those who earnestly seek him.* Hebrews 11:6

Feelings get pushed away too often, but I challenge you to test what you feel God is calling you to do. Get approval from God himself on things you wonder over your life. He wants you transformed, renewed, and growing in Him for all your days. If you have held yourself back from growth because of some past hurt, worldly set view, or major incident, I dare say test this belief out as Romans 12:2 suggests. Do as Hebrews 11:6 says and be faithful while earnestly calling on God to show you the truth of your own self.

E= EFFECTIVE plan: first look for trends...where do you find yourself getting stuck? What do you avoid? When do you hear yourself do negative self-talk? When do you feel insecure? What is an accomplishment you'd love to succeed in but never try or never reach? When do you find yourself acting out, losing patience? Do you keep asking for repentance over the same transgression? Is there some negative aspect of your life you keep reliving? Your plan needs to be specific to you. Step by step, one trial at a time, we recognize and replace- replacing the bad with what is **good and right**! This is an awesome technique I use regularly with great success.

RECOGNIZE & REPLACE

A good example of this is a woman I coached who is definitely one of the most generous, helpful and joy-filled people I know, but she had blocks that kept her from moving on to more. She coped with her insecurities for advancing by remaining in her current place. By the time she was wrapping up her coaching she was ready to move past this foot hold.

Much of her inhibitions came from fear of making mistakes, and looking incapable. She had been emotionally abused by her father that she loved very much. One particular sentence he said to her as a child now had roots so deep that they held her down far stronger than she was even aware of. The sentence, "I am not real sure which you are, more helpless or hopeless." I found this so odd because she came off completely opposite of this to me. But it was 'her truth' and I knew it held much power in her life.

We did a lot of coaching on what is good and right, what the Bible tells us is true, and we came up with a replacement to the falsehood she now recognized. The new affirmation that would replace this toxic sentence was the complete opposite. It was of God and it was true. Every time she heard her mind affirm her old belief of "I don't know which you are, more helpless or hopeless?" she replaced it with "I don't know which you are, more helpful or hopeful."

She made efforts to follow through with one affirming behavior to this truth after each time she spoke the words. (This connects the emotional part of herself with the intellectual part of herself.) Each week we discussed how often she caught herself using the replacement sentence and what her step was.

Personal growth is heavily affected by awareness, making my role simple-offering clarity on the truth our Heavenly Father teaches us, and what is true and right. It didn't take long before she was plugging away on her own, and acting more and more in line with this new belief system of how God truly designed her as she is...extremely helpful and hopeful.

She said something that stuck with me, telling me how interesting it was that it took years of repeating the lie in her thoughts for her to find herself one day simply believing it; but that hearing and recognizing the truth of God's words and love for her -that wiped out the pain and control of the lies had held, almost overnight. This is the power of our Heavenly Father. All of His power is here for each of us, we simply need to tap into Him-letting truth and light take over the darkness.

C= COMBAT: These steps need to be specific toward you and your individual setbacks noted under the effective plan. First, you recognize your setbacks, as you did under "E" effective plan. Then you find ways to combat (replace) these footholds through the Word.

Finally, brothers and sisters, whatever is true, whatever is noble, whatever is right, whatever is pure, whatever is lovely, whatever is admirable--if anything is excellent or praiseworthy--think about such things. Philippians 4:8

Broad Steps to take when needing to REPLACE negative behavior/mindsets with positive ones.

- Get yourself surrounded by positive people and those who love and care for you.
- Engage in people who desire to bring you up and not tear you down.
- Learn Bible verses that specifically relate to your weaknesses. Carry them with you, write them in your planner, add them on your cell phone screen, or post them on your mirror in the bathroom.
- Pray to God asking Him to make you aware of areas you are judging yourself on or haven't let go of, and to see the damage it may be having on your life.
- Get Christian music or talk radio on the radio station verses secular music.
- Listen to sermons, audio Bible or podcasts as you work out or get ready in the morning.

T= TEST out your plan, (remember Romans 12:2 on testing) God teaches us to test out beliefs we may be unsure of. We need to be paying attention to the results…

- Are they in line with our Father's plan for us?
- Is the practice resulting in you carrying out God's laws better?
- Are you seeing heavenly blessings as a result?

You indeed are perfect today, as perfectly imperfect as you are supposed to be. You may lie down at night wishing you'd done a little better, but remind yourself that you are a child of the one true God, who is living and working in you. So your work today was just as it should be.

If you want more for your tomorrow, live in the hope and joy that God still lives and breathes in YOU. Give up your transgressions of today, thanking Jesus with all your heart for your renewed place. Then call on your Father to straighten your path, and to the Holy Spirit to guide you into a beautiful tomorrow.

THE GIFT

CHAPTER 7
ARE YOU RECEIVING UNCONDITIONAL LOVE?

PERFECTLY IMPERFECT

PERFECTLY IMPERFECT

THE GIFT

ARE YOU RECEIVING UNCONDITIONAL LOVE?

This chapter on considering the gift of seeing ourselves as perfectly imperfect shows just how much goodness will come of truly latching on to the ultimate gift of unconditional love. The need to know of God's deep love for you regardless of your flaws is so important and is why I chose to start the Living Legacy with my story of meeting my maker.

I was a sinner as I sat on that couch loving my sweet baby, yet I was still offered unconditional love and acceptance. I was welcomed in with love and sent back with love. I was left with one understanding of our purpose here, to love and be loved.

We need to be reassured that we are flawed and sinners but that is NOT **who** we are. We are children of the most high, fearfully and wonderfully made!

We may be sinning, possess imperfections and fail in various ways, but none of that matters within the Glory of God's grace through Jesus Christ, and **this is what we need to remember!**

> **Consider the Gift:** Unconditional love, acceptance, and eternal life.

What does the 'Word' tell us about God's gift of love offered to us all?

By His love we were predestined as His...

For he chose us in him before the creation of the world to be holy and blameless in his sight. In love he predestined us for adoption to sonship through Jesus Christ, in accordance with his pleasure and will— to the praise of his glorious grace, which he has freely given us in the One he loves. Ephesians 1:4-6

The gift of love offers so much more...

If receiving unconditional love and acceptance (despite your worst self) is not too much already, it is not your only gift. God has graced you with so much more, and He is just waiting for you to take it.

Not only so, but we also glory in our sufferings, because we know that suffering produces perseverance; perseverance, character; and character, hope. And hope does not put us to shame, because God's love has been poured out into our hearts through the Holy Spirit, who has been given to us. Romans 5:3-5

Consider the gift: Perseverance, hope and character.

There are many versions of this verse found within our various Christian Bibles. One says 'graced in our tribulation,' versus 'glory in our suffering,' or 'rejoice.' I find that translation using 'grace' very insightful and truly less likely for us to get confused with.

Have you or someone close to you had to endure something horrible or unbearable? Well, if we're not careful, this verse can make us feel like God **GIVES** us trials to make us better or stronger. And, that we somehow need to be happy that He does this **TO** us.

I have to stop and talk about this because so many people who I coach and who are working through a huge trial can end up feeling this way. They may feel they either need to learn something yet, so God did this to them so they will then be taught or they don't feel like they deserved whatever this horrible heartbreak is and wonder why God is almost punishing them.

This is so human, and real, and it's okay. It is part of moving through a process...but this is why we need to really know 'the Word.' Let's break it down.

Look at Romans 5:3-5 one more time. Do you see this verse to say 'God gives us trials' to ... **OR**, does the verse say 'He knows' about the trials? We know this as well, from day one He knew every move we would make. What He does for us is GRACES us with the gift of using these trials to somehow gain good. This is our gift, our true blessing of being a child of God.

> **Consider the gift:** God graces us with good out of our trials.

So why aren't we all living in the glory of our weaknesses or trials? Many of us are just plain suffering in them and this plainly breaks my heart.

What does it take for us to not live in our trials?

An energy shift is needed to put our hope in God and the future...

- I want us to focus on a shift of energy for this task of moving from suffering in our trials to gaining from our trials. This can take us to a place of hope for the gain that WILL come through the grace of God and by our blind faith. Depending on the severity of the trial, the faith involved is often a feat few can muster alone.

- This is what I help people do...learn deeply about the truths within our Bible related to their trial, to gain understanding and insight that will increase their blind faith in risking such abandonment of a real hurt that seems unbearable to let go of. I encourage them in a way God called me to, and teach them steps to 'move out of suffering and into hope.'
- This hope will carry them away from despair and into the light. This will grow and then they will someday look back at this suffering and see their growth. They will have an overwhelming appreciation for our Father giving them just what they needed to pull through and even bear fruit.

3 Truths for Progressing Out of Suffering and Despair and Into the Gifts of Hope and Blessings.

1. God did not DO this trial to you.

He IS waiting to grace you through it and bring glory to you from Him because of your faith and because He loves you.

For he chose us in him before the creation of the world to be holy and blameless in his sight. In love he predestined us for adoption to sonship through Jesus Christ, in accordance with his pleasure and will— to the praise of his glorious grace, which he has freely given us in the One he loves. Ephesians 1:4-6

2. Faith makes things possible, not easy.

Just because we adopt the right frame of mind with the trial, does not mean it will be easy. Hope and faith are the key, but we will still need to do our part of "Acting in faith."

In the same way, faith by itself, if it does not prove itself with actions, is dead. James 2:17

I like to explain faith and action like one of those desk toys that has a wooden base with a metal bar across the top. On this bar are strings with metal balls that are all lined up. They just sit there with loads of potential, if not ignited into movement.

Once an individual takes action and lifts one of the end balls- letting it drop to hit the next, momentum takes over and there is a chain reaction and off it goes.

The interesting thing is once it is ignited, it actually takes an individual to physically stop it or the energy from which it started will carry it through to the next act.

Consider the Gift: This is how God works. By our deeds of good faith, we spark a lifetime of action from the Almighty!

3. Hind sight is 20/20.

Throughout these chapters you have gotten a good look at God's gift of unconditional love FOR YOU, how you are adopted by God through your faith of Jesus Christ bearing your sins-for your eternal glory, and because of these two gifts you then may allow yourself to have hope for the future regardless of your trials.

And now these three remain: faith, hope and love. But the greatest of these is love. 1 Corinthians 13:13

Hope is not the only gift this unconditional love and 'perfectly imperfect' view of self will provide…because with love of self and others comes so much more: grace, tolerance, and compassion. Do you ever wonder why God says, "Of these, faith, hope and love, the most important is love"? It is because He is love, and He is all things good. When love is in us, He is in us. When He is in us, His goodness is in us and all that encompasses it.

"I am the vine; you are the branches. If you remain in me and I in you, you will bear much fruit; apart from me you can do nothing." John 15:5

> **Consider the Gift:** Do we think of gifts in terms other than material pleasures?…What are some gifts you have received as a result of your trials and hardships?
>
> Bear much fruit: grace, tolerance, and compassion.

Hope ~ Grace ~ Tolerance ~ Compassion

Now, I truly appreciate these years of great struggle in reading and writing, and yes, I do in fact have to work very hard at it to this day. But it's the gift I gained from it which has me praising the Lord. I am a hard worker, I listen well, and have very good problem solving skills. Each trait is a direct result of having this learning disorder.

"Never overlook the good in a bad situation."
- Zig Ziglar

THE CHOICE

CHAPTER 8
ARE YOU IN A PERFECT PLACE?

PERFECTLY IMPERFECT

PERFECTLY IMPERFECT

THE CHOICE

ARE YOU IN A PERFECT PLACE?

In all growth there is a place where you have to make a decision. In the 'Consider a Choice' chapter for being perfectly imperfect, we learn how it isn't enough to simply understand this process for learning to love your God, others, and yourself as God made you. For real change and transformation, we need to decide on owning the truth about ourselves, and acting on it in faith within the Glory of God.

**Do I move forward and change,
or do I stay here and wait?**

Waiting for what? Here we take a hard look at the partnership of accountability and growth. Some of our most amazing individuals found themselves in a place of accountability for their growth. Imagine their life had they not decided to move forward in faith and passion.

Beethoven for example, a magnificent musician who had lost his hearing, Helen Keller; a deaf and blind leader for positivity and grit; Oprah Winfrey, a victim of sexual abuse and now one of the world's strongest female leaders.

If we can have faith in the truth of our Heavenly Father's craftsmanship as He built us and works on us, we will soar with a strength beyond our understanding. We will reach heights we once dared not to believe and we will carry on with energy and passion that does not grow weary.

but those who trust in the LORD will renew their strength. They will soar on wings like eagles; they will run and not grow weary, they will walk and not be faint. Isaiah 40:31

Energy beyond our understanding...

When we really own the understanding that we are perfectly imperfect, our difficulties no longer works on us-having been wiped away by grace. We are then only left with the results for our disciplined behavior from God's molding of us and work in us. When we are full of acceptance, hope, and strength it ignites a passion for growth. We no longer will be comfortable living in the pain, hurt, or destruction of our trials.

Think about any past hurts, trials, or setbacks that you are still living in. Jot down on a piece of paper just how this trial is having an E.F.F.E.C.T. on your life. Think about what your life would be like if those hurts, trials or setbacks were completely gone.

For the time will come when people will not put up with sound doctrine. Instead, to suit their own desires, they will gather around them a great number of teachers to say what their itching ears want to hear. 4 They will turn their ears away from the truth and turn aside to myths. 2 Timothy 4:3-4

I want so badly for you and everyone to find sanctification through Christ, regardless of your upbringing, history, or relationship with God up to this point. God knows exactly where you are at today and wants you washed clean and hopeful for your future living in the benefits of a healthy clean life that only Christ and God can offer.

Sometimes I have clients who hold themselves back from growth because they can't imagine or see themselves in the pure (washed clean way), and I understand that. I like to use a child of their own, if they have one, as an example. We often can love our child a little more Christ-like than anyone else, even ourselves.

Think about a time when one of your children, or someone very close to you, struggled with a bad setback. Addiction, disability, or a big mistake. Did you love them any less? And we are nowhere near as loving as God is. Doing this little experiment helps us to see how God is waiting to love us through our sin and imperfections.

This is one of my favorite Christian songs on loving with God's eyes. Look at these lyrics written by Brandon Heath. Oh, if we could all just have eyes like our Father, we would not so quickly write others off; and to be honest, even to write ourselves off.

Give me Your eyes for just one second, give me Your eyes so I can see.

Everything that I keep missing, give me Your love for humanity.

Give Me Your Eyes, What If We Album, 2008 Brandon Heath

(Here is the YouTube link to watch the video: www.youtube.com/watch?v=P5AkNqLuVgY)

Consider the Choice: Increased patience, grace and peace from the compassionate and loving eyes of our Father or judgment and measure most easily seen with worldly eyes. It's up to us.

The Inside-Out Process

(from Chapter 5 'Consider the Problem')

This song is an excellent example of the gift of compassion that's received from the love of God in our hearts, minds, and souls. As we begin to let more and more of God's love into our hearts, we are more and more capable of loving others in a more Christ-like way.

Aren't we tired yet of judging others, with no clue as to how or why they are who they are? God knows. Isn't that enough? This is human, I know, but with a heart after God, living in God, and God in you, the purer your love will become.

Seeing the world through God's eyes, as in 'Give Me Your Eyes' by Branden Heath, speaks this understanding so well. He is on an airplane, and by seeing the world as a creation from afar, his faith comes to fruition. As a once non-believer, he now walks off the airplane as a Christian. He sees people, not busyness.

He sees their fear, shame, and doubt as people pass, while others merely breeze along their busy day. He understands that he was just like the other preoccupied airport occupants. He now sings with all his passion the desire to "see more." That is how it works!

When we see ourselves through God's eyes, we are slowly able to see more of God's great work in our self and with it the ability to be and do more.

As we see others through God's eyes, we then slowly see them in a more loving and compassionate way. In turn this will provide us with more patience, grace, and peace. This is a powerful transformation!!!

What is this transformation that Christ and Our Father offer?

Create in me a clean heart, O God, And renew a steadfast spirit within me. Psalm 51:10

Rid yourselves of all the offenses you have committed, and get a new heart and a new spirit. Why will you die, people of Israel? Ezekiel 18:31

I will give you a new heart and put a new spirit in you; I will remove from you your heart of stone and give you a heart of flesh. Ezekiel 36:26

We love because he first loved us. 1 John 4:19

Before we move on to Part Three, we have one last choice to consider in relation to our lives being perfectly imperfect.

Does concealing transgressions (imperfections, wrong doings, sins) actually keep us from prospering? Absolutely.

Biblically we are called to be wise to our own transgressions.

Whoever conceals their sins does not prosper, but the one who confesses and renounces them finds mercy. Proverbs 28:13

When I coach people, I see this firsthand, over and over again. I witness it in my own life, and I see loved ones do this. It's rather painful and heartbreaking, but I believe no one is stuck in a bad place because they want to be. Too often we don't even realize we are stuck. I say it all the time, and I probably need to change my terminology but, "No one wants to be a stuck schmuck."

But seriously, I believe with all of my heart that we truly are doing the best we can, with the tools we have, and the insight bestowed within. We cannot change the way we were brought up or taught thus far, we cannot change the decisions we have made to get us where we are today. **We can, however, learn and grow.**

If we have an area of weakness and call on God for help, confide in fellow Christians, friends or family, they will surely help. Sometimes we find we need more education or training to help us move through our setbacks. We may go to our pastor, a coach, or someone else. We understand we need something to move forward, and we take steps to work through it. **This isn't the problem.**

The real problem is when we don't see our transgressions. My deepest growth has come from being moved to first see my true weaknesses. We need complete transparency with our self to see and admit our own weaknesses. I do not believe people desire to not grow or learn. I think they have no idea that they have areas that need growth or they have no idea how to learn newly needed skills.

This is one of the most valuable parts of life coaching, self-awareness. For the most part people want to be amazing and they would if they knew how. The very first step I take with my clients is completing and reviewing an intake form. This is a full session on self-awareness. I find it amazing that most individuals learn more in their first session then in weeks of meeting, because of all the enlightenment.

I loved the humility of one particular coaching client. She had a failed marriage that with a lot of hard work and honesty, she came to the understanding that she had left God to please her husband or to save herself the battle of fighting for faith in her marriage.

She had no idea of the cost this decision was having on her life as she was living it. She admits now how being away from church and the Word made it even simpler to mistakenly drift away. Once she came to this understanding, affirmed in her mind God's love for her even after this transgression, she raised it up to Him on bent knees and recommitted her life to her Father, partnering with Him once again, and ever since sings praises of joy over God's acceptance and unconditional love He showed her. He has blessed her abundantly in every sense and she is an unwavering woman of God that I am impressed with and so joyful over.

We need to pray for insight, pray for humble wisdom, pray to allow ourselves to be honest with our self. You are loved, so accept where you are. If you want 'better' for tomorrow, God has written that you simply need to reveal your transgressions, confess that truth to God, and ask for mercy and guidance. He will give it to you, and He will help you move to a place where at last you can prosper.

> **Consider the choice:** Which do you want... transparency that provides mercy, healing and growth or concealed transgressions for limited growth and abundance?

PART 3
WISE CHOICES WORK

THE PROBLEM

CHAPTER 9

WHAT MOTIVATES YOUR DECISION MAKING?

WISE CHOICES WORK

WISE CHOICES WORK

THE PROBLEM

WHAT MOTIVATES YOUR DECISION MAKING?

> It is hard navigating in this world right now. Beliefs are somehow getting mixed up with truths. How can we make a sound decision, how can we truly discern, if we no longer even know what the truth is?

Take a minute to think on the commonly used 10-point pain scale with 1 being the least amount of pain and 10 the most. If a person rates their pain as a 6, then it is a 6. It is their reality, and the healthcare team treats them appropriately. Now the very next person can have the exact same amount of injury put upon them, yet they score it a 4, which is their reality and they are treated appropriately.

The scale is very effective and proven. Even with varying impressions of pain stimuli, it works. It works because the tool in which pain is measured, is the same for everyone.

What if a patient used the pain scale backward, with 10 being the least? Or, what if an individual decided to make up their own scale, which wasn't used by the healthcare team at all? Chaos and pain would result.

Are those in and of God on the same playing field (moral compass) as those in and of the world?

For peak performance, we need to have those involved working off the same reference point. Work places do this with their Mission, Vision and Values. Many families do this as well, even having a contract to sign in agreement of house rules and conduct.

Consider the problem: Is our contract no longer visible, been rewritten or designed into a more eye and body appealing way?

The world has become more mobile, is reaching farther, and has more and more avenues for growth and resources. I see the once crisp black and white agreements and tools of our past are getting copied, and worn, and rewritten, and redesigned. Many good-intentioned neighbors, loved ones, and even ourselves at times, are off living life by a copy of a copy.

There are so many preachers on television leading masses to the Lord and churches are popping up everywhere... this is good-right?

Is it really any different from years past?

The Historical religious demographics of the United States, notes the number of documented Christians in the United States in 1950 at a whopping 91%, while in 2015 the number sadly lands at 70%. Of these, how many do you think are practicing Christians? My heart breaks for all those people who know not, and will not be reached.

We are a busy, mobile nation. We strive for efficiency and convenience. We need to 'fill-up' emotionally, because we literally drain ourselves with burnout and being stretched too thin and at the cost of our own lives.

The majority of my coaching clients are women in this very situation. They are doing their best to work fulltime, make good money, and feel responsible to keep their job. They are carting kids around to every activity under the sun, doing all they can to give their children the opportunities that are available. They keep the house, help with homework at night, and often have aging parents to add into the mix.

We go-go-go, and while this rat race is on, we prioritize. Sleep is often the place to cut from and this only packs on the pounds and wears these folks out more. Sunday is often the only day to catch up on sleep and rest. Church is often left out, not by intention but by what they feel is survival.

Little by little, piece by piece, the once black and white wisdom, written for all to live in and love by, is getting lost, faded... and buried. Our busy lives are crowding out church with it's Biblical teaching and the boundaries of good and bad, right and wrong, which are slowly muddying. This distance only carries away our empty souls, making it even harder to fill them up and restore our bones.

Years ago, in the 50's, 91% of us were spirituality infused with the Word as we faithfully loaded up our families and went to church. At church we wind down and focus on our message. We get fellowship, music, praise, worship, support, confession, love and communion all in one place. It is our gathering place. We were filled with the

> **Consider the Problem:** Are we so busy that we choose to cut out church? How many of us read the Bible? There is so much wisdom, and restoration found in it's black & white pages. If we need to prioritize, is church and its support the thing to cut?
>
> *This will bring health to your body and nourishment to your bones.* Proverbs 3:8

Word-restoring our mind, heart, and soul. At church the Word falls on solid ground and fertile soil.

Now, nearly 20% of these people are gone and missing their weekly planting and fertilizing-left to start a new week even emptier-with no replenishing.

They may hear wisdom and grace scattered among the day on a Christian radio station or posting that inspires them, but it is mixed among buzzing traffic and other social platforms. I wonder how likely these snippets of faith land on fertile ground as individuals are often multitasking, while their minds are still racing as the busyness surrounds them? (Thus God's request to never fail to meet together.)

> *It is a vicious cycle to get out of the habit of meeting. To become self reliant to the point of isolation.*

I do love all the technology these times have to offer (podcasts, blogs, Bible studies and Christian music). But how much of our Christian faith, in this busy mobile world, is based on self? We may be diligent enough to infuse our hearts, minds and souls into good and right teaching on our own. We may even hold our family up to catching a service together all cuddled up on the couch, sharing in faith, family, and home. We have done this many times ourselves-yet steering clear of a habit.

I warn you of routine, and convenience. God tells us time and time again to be in fellowship with each other.

> *not giving up meeting together, as some are in the habit of doing, but encouraging one another—and all the more as you see the Day approaching.* Hebrews 10:25

Consider the problem: Is the Christian faith based on individual station, worship and praise, or is it also based on unity, support, community and fellowship?

Let the message of Christ dwell among you richly as you teach and admonish one another with all wisdom through psalms, hymns, and songs from the Spirit, singing to God with gratitude in your hearts. Colossians 3:16

Our churches need to keep up with the times and be mindful of staying true to God's request of meeting together. The fellowship of meeting together gives Christians a place for spurring their faith and growth to take root. If we aren't around to hear the 'Word' as written, and to understand the story told, it too often falls on rocky ground.

Then he told them many things in parables, saying: "A farmer went out to sow his seed. As he was scattering the seed, some fell along the path, and the birds came and ate it up. Some fell on rocky places, where it did not have much soil. It sprang up quickly, because the soil was shallow. But when the sun came up, the plants were scorched, and they withered because they had no root. Matthew 13:3-6

WHAT IN THE WORLD CAN WE DO ABOUT IT?

Sometimes, not knowing what to do is our biggest problem. I call this Analysis Paralysis, and I coach many on this very topic. (See Chapter 10)

Analysis paralysis or paralysis by analysis is the state of over-analyzing (or over-thinking) a situation so that a decision or action is never taken, in effect paralyzing the outcome. https://en.wikipedia.org/wiki/Analysis_paralysis

> **Consider the Problem:** Do we even recognize this decline of practicing Christians? Do we recognize the significance of how we are practicing our faith today? Good and bad truly affects our lives and our nation.

I think it is important to be informed and to evaluate with a heart after God. This will do wonders. I included statistics into this concern so the 20% of lost Christians practicing their faith was not overlooked. This helps us acknowledge what is really taking place. Then I go on to list some reasons why I fear this has happened. Because these are already folks once embedded into a practice of church habits, I can only imagine this decline is more a result of innocence rather than malice. That's a little scary, the idea of losing our connection to our faith being one of innocence...slowly chipping away at our conviction and earnest commitment to God and His desires.

Call me an optimist, but I believe with the acknowledgment of how simple it is for this busy world to take root over our once firmly planted love and commitment for God, we will be wise by keeping the Holy Spirit close to our heart, mind and soul. Even as an individual backslides, they will feel nudges from the Holy Spirit, obey the call they hear, and make efforts to re-ignite their heart, mind, and soul with the power, faith, and healing that only God can offer. They will recognize all the support and growth that their church will provide not only themselves, but their family as well. I want this one chapter to reach down deep into the heart of those who hear these words.

HOW IN LINE ARE OUR PRACTICES TODAY?

To best recognize how we may have drifted from God's written request of us...

Let's consider how close we are to living our lives in the truth and the light...

WORK: In today's world we find ourselves guarded about speaking our faith too much, so as not to offend or infringe. We even do it at the risk of our safety these days, which I never thought I would say. This is the very reason why I find myself more vocal. We have to take a stand and do what we can to shine a light so bright that the darkness is snuffed out.

Not everyone is in a work environment where speaking openly about their faith is allowed. How well can we then do what is asked of us?

Whatever you do, work at it with all your heart, as for the Lord, not for human masters, Colossians 3:23

- **Be an example of Christ:** This is a true passion of mine, and I have quickly found it to be a huge blessing. I spent years leading in a setting where we were held to work as working for the Lord, in my eyes. We called it, 'Doing the right thing.' 'The Golden Rule.' Our standards of practice included being kind and respectful, compassionate and responsive-not unlike how God asks us to behave.
- **Make an intentional decision and work at it:** Because I have a private practice, I chose to move forward with faith at the forefront of my practice. It works wonderfully and I feel really good about it. As a Christian functioning within the public sector, walking like one will be most effective in your work-life. I reassure clients of this with two commands. First, love your God before no others. Second, love your neighbor as yourself. This is an awesome way to carry God to your workplace. The point is, both of these are great. You will need to figure out which is best for you...THEN COMMIT, live intentionally from here on out to do this.

HOME: In today's world we are pressured to do more and be more. We want to give our children every opportunity to succeed, so we teach them the ways of the busy world.

So then, are we spending more time and energy teaching them the ways of the world or the ways of God?

By wisdom a house is built, and through understanding it is established; through knowledge its rooms are filled with rare and beautiful treasures. Proverbs 24:3-4

NEIGHBOR: In today's world we scarcely know our neighbor and often run in and out of our homes with a to-do list scrolling around in our mind as we slip from car to house to car... So how well can we then do what God asks of us?

The second is this: 'Love your neighbor as your-self.' There is no commandment greater than these. Mark 12:31

CHURCH: In today's world we have awesome podcasts and praise music at our finger-tips, we have lake homes and many have money for travel... So how convenient is it to do what God asks of us?

And over all these virtues put on love, which binds them all together in perfect unity. Let the peace of Christ rule in your hearts, since as members of one body you were called to peace. And be thankful. Let the message of Christ dwell among you richly as you teach and admonish one another with all wisdom through psalms, hymns, and songs from the Spirit, singing to God with gratitude in your hearts. And whatever you do, whether in word or deed, do it all in the name of the Lord Jesus, giving thanks to God the Father through him. Colossians 3:14-17

THE WORD

CHAPTER 10
WHAT PROCESS WORKS?

WISE CHOICES WORK

THE WORD

WHAT PROCESS WORKS?

In this chapter I will share with you a 4-step process for making wise decisions and moving forward with God's power on your side. Using the Bible, God's living Word, to apply this 4-Step process is the very foundation of the 'Learning Legacy,' one of my main coaching programs.

1. Determine the purpose of the decision
2. Determine the need for compromise by the decision
3. Determine the potential results received by the decision
4. Determine the source of any fear of the decision

I have come to love and appreciate all this process has to offer. As with much of the growth of my practice, I came upon this by chance. More appropriately spoken- I came upon it through God's divine working. This process started as a random step I gave one particular client, and it worked. I tweaked it and improved it as I used it on different people, until one day it became the wonderful universal practice I use all the time and on most everyone.

If anyone doubts starting a new venture in the hands of God and wonders just how prepared they are, I have to say I simply stepped out in faith, prayed a lot, acted and tweaked.

Much of my whole practice started with a simple step, and I had to get used to being an amateur. (But an amateur with the most amazing trainer, leader, encourager, and supporter around, the Almighty.)

I started with catchy programs I'd learned of in my certification, the goal setting was second nature after years of doing it for patients and employees, I did many videos which worked fine, but I am pretty sure it was more the heart behind my coaching that did the heavy lifting. (And boy, if you want a few good belly laughs, go check out some of those first videos…I've even considered making a bloopers.)

But, it was late February of 2016 when I really started to listen to God, and acting on His Living Word with a very committed purpose.

Don't get me wrong, from the beginning I had stepped out in faith on this venture. I felt a great calling to do what I can to serve God and his people, my sisters and brothers. I understand that I am flawed and unworthy and at the same time capable and blessed to have joined up with our Father who will lead you and me to a great place.

From the second I considered my own coaching practice called, *"Fulfill Your Legacy,"* it has become my God given passion, with a purpose of leading others to their best place. Knowing how to make wise choices is crucial for advancement and growth, regardless of how good our intentions are.

How Did the 4 Steps Process for Decision Making Come To Be?

On April 6, 2016, my blog post was about making wise choices. I wrote it because one very special client named Kari kept asking me to help her make a sound decision. Now of course, I wouldn't make the decision for her, but I heard her plea and recognized her love for her faith. It sounds silly that I needed some epiphany to come to this understanding. But, if she really wanted answers, I'd been here before.

At that moment I knew where to direct her, and with a familiar whisper in my ear, I sent her to the 'Word.'

It almost got comical, as she found answer upon answer among the once forgotten pages of our 'Book.' She started challenging me with all of her big life questions and decisions, but I just kept directing her back to the 'Word.'

I found myself surprised with its clarity and insight that adapted to any need, any hurt, all questions, and soon I developed a pattern for finding clarity that was always enough, always right, always kind, loving, direct and gracious.

It's really rather simple and its success lies more in one taking action and using it. Let's turn to the Word when faced with big and small decisions.

What Is This 4-Step Process on Decision Making

1. **Determine the purpose of the decision.... Does one path lead with a purpose that serves God or gives glory to God in a way that is in alignment with your core values? If not, consider its wisdom or lack there of.**
   "So, whether you eat or drink, or whatever you do, do all to the glory of God." 1 Corinthians 10:31

2. **Determine the need for compromise by either decision... Does one path require you to align with key people who are not equally yoked with your values? Don't overlook good and right.**
   "Do not be unequally yoked with unbelievers. For what partnership has righteousness with lawlessness? Or what fellowship has light with darkness?" 2 Corinthians 6:14 ESV

3. **Determine the potential results received by each decision...Is one more aligned with your values? If by one action you do harm, or neglect what is good-and of God... think twice.**

Finally, brothers and sisters, whatever is true, whatever is noble, whatever is right, whatever is pure, whatever is lovely, whatever is admirable —if anything is excellent or praiseworthy—think about such things. Philippians 4:8

4. **Determine your fear...Is it fear of God and the power and strength He has to catapult you into more than you believe for yourself, or is it fear of the dark holding you back? Are your values resting on your omnipotent, omnipresent, omniscient loving God or on worldly gain or attraction to self serving fulfillment?...**
"Trust in the Lord with all of your heart and do not lean on your own understanding. In all your ways submit to Him, and He will make your paths straight." Proverbs 3:5-6.

Consider The Word: *For everything that was written in the past was written to teach us, so that through the endurance taught in the Scriptures and the encouragement they provide we might have hope.* Romans 15:4

THE GIFT

CHAPTER 11

WHAT COULD YOU GAIN, WHAT COULD YOU LOSE?

WISE CHOICES WORK

WISE CHOICES WORK

THE GIFT

WHAT COULD YOU GAIN, WHAT COULD YOU LOSE?

The Law of Cause & Effect states that absolutely everything happens for a reason. All actions (choices we make to proceed with) have consequences and produce specific results, as do all inactions. It's highly valuable to consider not just the effect of our actions, but also the source of our actions. Cause and effect are worldly laws which God is a part of. God, however, is more than this world; He is in, of and above this world.

In this chapter's opening sentence, think about the word 'reason.' That is what God is all about. He handles the behind the scenes effects of our actions. He knows the reasons we do things, and we receive blessings and teaching based on our motive or reason...this is far more significant in life than the simple worldly effects of our actions.

While coaching I sometimes encounter clients who question how sometimes people who say they are nonbelievers appear to have such a blessed life. This chapter, "Consider The Gift on Making Wise Choices," is dedicated to conveying the concept of actions and reactions happening in a two-fold formula.

We are all familiar with the cause and effect of the world, so this chapter will be focusing on joining up with God for your decisions, your actions, and your day to day life.

> **Consider the Gift:** With God as part of our decisions, we receive a response to our actions that is greater than that of which just the world can offer.

Stephen Baldwin Testimony

I like to have quick tools and resources for my clients, and Stephen Baldwin's Testimony is one I use frequently. It's a perfect example of someone so blessed by worldly standards-a successful actor, beautiful wife and children, and very wealthy. He lived freely and had many positive and negative effects of this lifestyle. He battled with addiction and much more.

However, it wasn't until he gave himself to Christ, he says 'born again,' that he truly feels blessed. Now his actions are done with the living God in him and his blessings he says are richer and go deeper than anything he ever knew before. He is doing Christian films now and changing lives everywhere. His impact is reaching far beyond himself and his family. He is abiding in the Living Legacy.

"Through the gratitude that I have, it's a privilege to know the Lord, to know the Word of God, to have the Spirit of God living inside of me. And it's a gift for me to have the opportunity to share it with other people. And I love it."
Stephen Baldwin Testimony

Stephen Baldwin Testimony
Please click the provided link for a quick YouTube video on his story with videos to follow on guest speaking he has done in much more detail. http://bit.ly/29b8C49

What I really like about his short testimonial is that he touched on a few key points. One being that God, the Word, and the Holy Spirit were living in him through Christ. The second, his feelings of peace, happiness, and immense gratitude for such a gift.

When making wise choices, I know there are two key elements we need to agree on. The first, is that true wisdom includes God, the Word and the Holy Spirit. The next element is a need to 'know' 'self.'

Consider the Gift: Peace and happiness, being able to know and love the one true God personally, to know the living Word that provides so much insight, to have the Holy Spirit inside of us and then be able to offer this most amazing gift to anyone.

We have free will to make our decisions. Let's be wise to who we are and where we need to call on God for insight and guidance.

Knowing yourself is the beginning of all wisdom. ~Aristotle

FREE WILL & TWO FOLD WISDOM

TWO FOLD WISDOM # 1 KNOWING THERE ARE TWO WORLDS & IT'S OUR FREE WILL TO CHOOSE!

- *THE LOVING WORLD OF GOD*
- *THE SINFUL WORLD OF EVIL*

Aristotle's quote used to bother me. Shouldn't knowing God be the beginning of all wisdom? But, as I am working with people who are simply doing their best to make wise choices and come to better places in life, I have come to understand the significance of our flesh here on earth.

Do not love the world or anything in the world. If anyone loves the world, love for the Father[a] is not in them. For everything in the world—the lust of the flesh, the lust of the eyes, and the pride of life—comes not from the Father but from the world. The world and its desires pass away, but whoever does the will of God lives forever. 1 John 2:15-17

LOVING THE WORLD

(But how can this be bad... God so loved the world?)

- When we are told *not* to love things of the world, the Bible is referring to the world's corrupt value system. Satan does have power here and acts as the god of this world. This corrupt value system contradicts all that we know is right with God and His ways. It's the things of the world that interfere and distract us from our love for God.

The god of this age has blinded the minds of unbelievers, so that they cannot see the light of the gospel that displays the glory of Christ, who is the image of God. 2 Corinthians 4:4

- How can we know which world we are loving? Our God loves this world, and we know He loves us. He gives us blessings here which are of this world. I like to consider 1 John 2:16. Satan's system works off of three main evils...
  - the lust of the flesh.
  - the lust of the eyes.
  - the boastful pride of life.

*Every sin imaginable stems from them...envy, adultery, lying, selfishness, and more grow from those three roots.

For everything in the world—the lust of the flesh, the lust of the eyes, and the pride of life—comes not from the Father but from the world. 1 John 2:16

- Mental check: When we love the world, we are devoted to the world's treasures, philosophies, and priorities.

No one can serve two masters, for either he will hate the one and love the other, or he will be devoted to the one and despise the other. You cannot serve God and money. Matthew 6:24

This is talking about serving, and yes, I absolutely believe this. Where is our motive behind the things we do and the work we do? That's the quickest way to assess who we are serving. Are you motivated by all things good and loving? Or, is the root of your motivation money, self serving, or fame?

LOVING THE LORD

Again, we know we are to love the Lord and let him dwell in us. As we do that, we become more Christ like. We thankfully have Christ because God asks for us to keep His commands, and we will fall short at times. But, it is still His desire that we try. Love grows, so with God in our hearts, we are able to do better each day, which then results in heavenly blessings… abiding in what I call the Living Legacy.

For I command you today to love the Lord your God, to walk in obedience to him, and to keep his commands, decrees and laws; then you will live and increase, and the Lord

> **Consider the Gift:** Heavenly Blessings, no more torment or fear, continued growth.

your God will bless you in the land you are entering to possess. Deuteronomy 30:16

- Goodbye to fear and torment when walking with the Lord. When we walk with the Lord, we get His protection. For if God be with you, who can be against you?

There is no fear in love. But perfect love drives out fear, because fear has to do with punishment. The one who fears is not made perfect in love. 1 John 4:18

- We then become more loving... Another reminder that God knows we are NOT perfect, but He wants us striving for it! He makes it possible for us to become more loving as our days, when lived in Him, are carried out.... abiding in the Living Legacy. Perfection of love.

This is how love is made complete among us... 1 John 4:17

TWO FOLD WISDOM #2 KNOWING OURSELVES ENOUGH TO NOT FALL PREY & IT'S OUR FREE WILL TO CHOOSE

These bodies of ours want to act on their own and we need to know ourselves in order to combat against our very own flesh.

Those who trust in themselves are fools, but those who walk in wisdom are kept safe. Proverbs 28:26

Knowing ourselves helps us identify:
1. **WHERE** we are weak versus where we are strong.
2. **WHAT** will cause us stress or what will lift us up.
3. **WHEN** we will likely behave well and when we may let the flesh win.
4. **WHY** it helps us know who inspires our growth and who brings us down.

I do not understand what I do. For what I want to do I do not do, but what I hate I do. Romans 7:15

We don't always like to be transparent with ourselves, but it honestly makes all the difference. Think about it. If you truly cannot recognize your own weaknesses and transgressions you will not be able to give them to God, or let Christ do what he DIED to do for you...cleanse you from all unrighteousness.

Being transparent with our self first and then with God offering up our transgressions we get to reap the affects of Gods grace at work. If we fail to self evaluate, recognize our sins, and offer them up, we will not reap the rewards of the growth that is awaiting for us...let alone the undeniable blessings waiting as well.

The most amazing thing about the two-fold wisdom concept is that God works in both. All we need to do is call on Him. It is truly inspiring to know that all this wisdom is with in our reach. We simply need to ask!

What good are glasses if we don't wear them?
What use is wisdom if we don't open the book?

I spur you on to love God with all your heart, soul, and mind. To ask God to dwell in you, to guide and protect you. To seek all the knowledge and wisdom found in the Bible, God's living word. To sing praises for guidance that is given to you through the Holy Spirit! And Last, to give up your flesh and sinful ways to the Lord, living in an abundant and righteousness life through Christ.

~Abide in the Living Legacy~

THE CHOICE

CHAPTER 12
WHAT IS AHEAD, THE SKY IS THE LIMIT?

WISE CHOICES WORK

WISE CHOICES WORK

THE CHOICE

WHAT IS AHEAD,
THE SKY IS YOUR LIMIT?

Matthew 25:14-30, the 'story of the talents,' reinforces the need to be wise with your talents (blessings/gifts). God is expecting us to do good work, and He is trusting in us to do such work. He, the loving God, wants to reward us with more as we prove faithful with wise responses to his requests.

Can you imagine watching a child of yours who is gifted with great athleticism, around eighteen, stop practicing, start missing game after game, and end up sabotaging himself from what is clearly seen as a blessed future?

God hates to see us waste His talents and offerings too. He wants us to be blessed and to enjoy His blessings. As it is written, EVERYONE is gifted with some talent, so if you are feeling like you aren't sure what yours is, it might simply be tucked down under this busy world...and we need to do some work to let it out!

This talent or gift may be evident from birth, or it may be a small portion in comparison. We are asked to use it wisely either way. Then it will be multiplied for us to faithfully use it again and even more.

Much of my coaching is used on this matter, which can be seen by my devoting a whole part of this book to it. I have incorporated a practice of 'Faith Infused Living' with all of my coaching now.

It is my passion to get us all back into the day to day practice of using God, our faith, the Word, and our salvation to the best of our abilities. And, all in God's name! I want each and every one of you to live an abundant life in Christ and to give God the Glory while we are carrying out His wishes.

This 4-Part Faith-Infused Living practice used in each 'part' of this book and study contains a pattern of ...

- consider the problem
- consider the word
- consider the gift
- consider the choice

Let's look a little closer at the 4-part Faith Infused Living practice before making our ultimate choice on how engaged in our faith we want to be. I want you to really think how this practice of infusing faith into your daily life with any challenge or goal is life transforming.

There is nothing new about seeking God in a time of need. In fact, isn't that when we most often call on Him? Many will admit that it is in those difficult times that they really cry out to God and seek answers. Slowly I am learning to seek first, and to be what I call a proactive Christian! However, this chapter is asking even more of us.

God doesn't want us to just be proactive and seek Him first. He also wants us to be responsive to all He offers us.

> **Consider the Choice:** This Faith Infused Living that
> is TRULY a proactive and responsive part of our day
> to day lives <u>is a decision</u> to be accountable to what
> God asks of us each day...BEFORE we land in trou-
> ble. It's proactive Godly living.
> Proactive & Responsive or Reactive & Needy?

"Let's be Proactive & Responsive Christians!"

Now we know that whatever the Law says, it speaks to
those who are under the Law, so that every mouth may be
closed and all the world may become accountable to God;
Romans 3:19

This verse is said by Paul, with him making known God's
will as to man's conduct. When we own our faith, we become
His and He ours. God lives in us-it's a beautiful circle as we
live and grow and become more...and live more, grow more
and become more.

Faith Infused Living!

PROACTIVE:
1. Seek First:
   - **Own Him:** You are His & He is Yours
     ...just as He chose us in Him before the foundation of
     the world, that we would be holy and blameless before
     Him In love He predestined us to adoption as sons
     through Jesus Christ to Himself, according to the kind
     intention of His will, Ephesians 1:4-5

     I am the vine; you are the branches. Whoever abides
     in me and I in him, he it is that bears much fruit, for
     apart from me you can do nothing. John 15:5

- **Love Him:** Because He first loved us...
  And he said to him, "You shall love the Lord your God with all your heart and with all your soul and with all your mind. Matthew 22:37

- **Go to Him:** *But seek first the kingdom of God and his righteousness, and all these things will be added to you.* Matthew 6:33

- **Call to Him:** *"Then you will call upon me and come and pray to me, and I will hear you. You will seek me and find me, when you seek me with all your heart."* Jeremiah 29: 12-13

- **Study Him:** *My son, do not forget my teaching, but let your heart keep my commandments, for length of days and years of life and peace they will add to you. Let not steadfast love and faithfulness forsake you; bind them around your neck; write them on the tablet of your heart. So you will find favor and good success in the sight of God and man. Trust in the Lord with all your heart, and do not lean on your own understanding. ...* Proverbs 3:1-35

2. See with God's eyes:
   - **Forgiving:** *And forgive us our debts, as we also have forgiven our debtors..* Matthew 6:12

   - **Accepting:** *But the wisdom that comes from heaven is first of all pure; then peace-loving, considerate, submissive, full of mercy and good fruit, impartial and sincere.* James 3:17

   - **Encouraging:** *Therefore encourage one another and build each other up, just as in fact you are doing.* 1 Thessalonians 5:11

   - **Compassion:** *Therefore, as God's chosen people, holy and dearly loved, clothe yourselves with compassion, kindness, humility, gentleness and patience.* Colossians 3:12

3. Send thanks ahead of time: There is much talk about how God works, in terms of time. Many verses and scholarly teaching to give thanks for your requests in your prayers

as you SEND the prayer in faith…not as you RECEIVE the answer you want.

We know our life has been all mapped out. So regardless of how major the dilemma is we are shooting a prayer up for, it's been and is being answered in one way or another. AND, as we know how much God loves us and trust in this love, we know it will be answered in a manner to best serve us. To that I will always say thank you!

• Gratitude first: Thankful Prayers in faith

Therefore I tell you, whatever you ask in prayer, believe that you have received it, and it will be yours. Mark 11:24

RESPONSIVE:
1. Accountable:
   • **Learn** of, master, and use your gifts/talents:
     Each of you should use whatever gift you have received to serve others, as faithful stewards of God's grace in its various forms. 1 Peter 4:10

   • **Give Thanks** steadily:
     But thanks be to God, who in Christ always leads us in triumphal procession, and through us spreads the fragrance of the knowledge of him everywhere. For we are the aroma of Christ to God among those who are being saved and among those who are perishing, to one a fragrance from death to death, to the other a fragrance from life to life." 2 Corinthians 2:14-15 ESV

   • **Love,** of these the most important is love:
     We love because He first loved us. 1 John 4:19

   • **Serve,** make your life about serving others with a heart after God:
     Commit your work to the Lord, and your plans will be established. Proverbs 16:3

- **"Go,"** God commanded us to love and to go spread the good word-making disciples of all nations. He also gave us our talents to use wisely:
  Go and make disciples of all the nations, baptizing them in the name of the Father and of the Son and of the Holy Spirit, teaching them to observe all things that I have commanded you; and lo, I am with you always, even to the end of the age." Amen. Matthew 28:19-20

Consider the gift: Gifts/Talents/Blessings when used wisely gain and multiply. Being in and of God, increases your wisdom and ability to serve more fully.

PART 4
MISTAKES MATTER

THE PROBLEM

CHAPTER 13

WHAT IF YOU GAVE UP?

MISTAKES MATTER

Mistakes Matter

THE PROBLEM

WHAT IF YOU GAVE UP?

Did you know that penicillin was created by accident? Alexander Fleming was attempting to find a wonder drug for fighting infections, with repeated failed attempts. One day he noticed a bacteria-filled petri dish that had been tossed in the trash earlier was dissolving other bacteria all around it.

Fleming was working the very passion he felt was right for him...and he was failing.

He did find the cure, after failing over and over. Without those failed attempts all tossed into the trash, he wouldn't have been able to witness the true miracle of nature healing itself.

He found an amazing cure because he used a door opened to him. Something in him was alert and ready to notice what many would have blown by.

Do we miss the doors God is opening before us with our failed attempts? Do we stay diligent in our pursuit? Do we see one failed attempt and then think, surely God did not want it to happen?

What can we learn from Fleming's success?

How to Make Successes Out of Failures

Fleming's failed attempts were necessary

- We have to go forward and trust that we are learning as we make mistakes. No matter how foolish or incapable we may feel, when our goal is as noble as our desire to achieve it, God is with us and He is able to provide all we need to achieve.

    Do not be deceived: God cannot be mocked. A man reaps what he sows. Galatians 6:7

Fleming's willingness to stay engaged: his original goal or passion, even after failing, allowed him the possibility to achieve success in the end.

- Passion is the key. Fleming was passionate about finding this cure. He believed in it and would not give up.
- We need to remember how important it is to first only do things that we know are in line with God's direction or hope for us. After knowing that, then insure it is something that we are truly passionate about. This will keep us engaged through the tough times.

    Therefore, my dear brothers and sisters, stand firm. Let nothing move you. Always give yourselves fully to the work of the Lord, because you know that your labor in the Lord is not in vain. 1 Corinthians 15:58

Fleming expected success: remain optimistic as you fail, to be prepared for what's next, and wait expectantly for the victory!

- Hopefully waiting.

    "I wait for the LORD, my soul waits, and in his word I hope; my soul waits for the Lord more than watchmen for the morning, more than watchmen for the morning." 1 Corinthians 15:58

- I love this....'more than watchmen for the morning.' Think on that. Waiting like it's our job. A job that provides safety, duty and responsibility to others. We are not only supposed to wait on the Lord and all His works, but wait like it is our job. A job so important that lives are at stake based on how well we do. It's hard to not grow impatient while waiting on a dream you felt was 'right.' (One that you put your heart, mind and soul into.) But, our timing is not God's. Trust that it is written that He will answer your prayers; how or when may not be what you had in mind. But rest assured that your prayers, when done in faith and in His name, will be answered.
- Then take note of the first part of the verse- we wait with our souls in a hopeful place!
- Pray for doors to open, and for joy and hope while waiting.

I know how hard this can be. Starting *"Fulfill Your Legacy"* was quite a risk. Being so open in my faith made me feel vulnerable and raw; and keeping my full-time job for as long as I did was difficult physically and emotionally.

The most valuable advice I can offer anyone stepping out in faith is to be real with yourself and in your plans! Call on God whenever anything negative or harming tries to work its way into your heart, mind or soul! Make sure your plans are aligned with God's teaching and use your skills and blessings wisely.

Is there anything you would really like to do, any dream for your life, marriage, family, or work... but you hold yourself back, you doubt your ability, or you have tried but come up against resistance and tucked the hope, goal or dream away?

Sometimes it's not just that someone isn't in their right place...it has more to do with them taking their right place to a new level.

Fear of making mistakes, looking crazy or silly, not having enough strength, feeling vulnerable, or falling flat on our faces

Consider the Problem: Fear of making mistakes, looking crazy or silly, or falling flat on your face.

can be the precursor for not moving forward or for keeping us from venturing out onto a new path.

This is something that has surprised me while coaching folks on their goals and driving force: many people seem to be in their place of calling, but they haven't engaged themselves into their full potential. They haven't allowed themselves to go deep, to really join up with God and to see where this conviction can take them.

There are two individuals I know that come to mind when I think of them being in their place of calling, and how far more fulfilling and life changing their work is for themselves and those they serve now, because of the deeper place and commitment.

> **Consider the Problem:** Could some of us be in our place of calling but we haven't quite partnered with God in this journey?

Jane

One is a nurse; we will name her Jane. She came to me ready to quit nursing, stating she was 'burnt out.' She wondered if she should find a job where she didn't need to be around people, or for sure not caring for them. While working through her intake assessment and several obstacles, I learned she had had the same boss for 15 years, and just over 3 years ago she had gotten a new one. There were many changes with the new boss including nursing hours and job culture.

The work environment was very direct, dutiful and independent. She liked much of that, being a stickler for details, but found herself lonely and had not gotten a good nights sleep for a few years, now that her hours were different. She was also only able to attend church every other weekend now, and had slowly drifted away from her normal religious practices.

She found herself reacting negatively to work pressures and had little time to engage with the patients. I helped her develop a plan to give her current job a chance, as she mentioned she had never thought to approach her boss, and hadn't even realized much of her frustration rooted from the change in her environment more than her actual work.

After a few months with some changes her boss had put into place, she found her right place at work again. She was in awe of her misplaced understanding of what the problem really was, and was so relieved to be loving her job and life again-even saying she loved it even more.

Based on seniority she got moved to one weekend a month, and they rearranged some scheduling practices to allow halls to work together. She attends church three out of four weekends a month now, and has physical and emotional support from her coworkers. She appreciates what she almost lost and goes the extra mile for her patients. She no longer just brings them their pills and provides cares of daily living; she embraces them as sisters and brothers in Christ, loving them each and doing all she can to make a difference in their days personally.

She knows and understands them better now and is privately praying for them, something she'd never really thought of before but loves it and truly feels it makes a difference. Jane is in her sweet spot...she is abiding in the living legacy.

Mr. Bolluyt

Mr. Bolluyt deserves a section in this book. There are certain individuals who carry on in their work day making it evident to others that they are in their calling. I included this example in order to stress how effective we can be when working our God-given gift in an environment where open religious practices are not acceptable.

Mr. Bolluyt was my favorite high school teacher. He did not just teach us skills. He knew how we learned, knew our personalities and picked up on troubles one may be having. He asked questions and reached out to offer any assistance he could. He cared. He was a just man and would notice if someone was being treated unfairly. If they were, regardless if it were by another teacher or by a peer, he would hold others up to correcting any wrong doing. He was a kind, wonderful man, witnessing to me a Godly man.

I do not know his personal beliefs on faith, but I do know he inspired me to be a good and right person, he taught me algebra, which I probably forgot every piece of, but his heart...I will never forget that.

This is what I want for my clients...for them to find themselves assured that their current place of work is their God given life purpose, and to deeply engage in it... or for them to recognize for the first time their God given life purpose and to know how to get it.

Working with clients who want help finding their God-given life purpose and helping them take steps to put it into action is one of the most fulfilling parts of my job. They start plugging away at their gifts, talents, and dreams, and I help them work on a solid plan. This plan includes a lot of self realization practices, inspiring them to work through their growth, and encouraging them to risk making mistakes, with the knowledge that God has their back. Teaching them how to use all that God and the 'Word' has to offer is so fulfilling. I simply love watching their transformation, and seeing them begin to live their days in the sweet spot abiding in the living legacy!

So What Keeps Us From Diving Deep?

So what keeps us from going deep, from trying new things, from risking short term failure as we step out in faith? Most often it's a foothold on our progression that can originate **internally or externally.** Either way, both are an act of Satan making us the victim, and neither are of God.

INTERNAL VICTIM: Fear and doubt only comes from the enemy. God is love. God gives peace, support, strength and protection. We need to keep our internal thoughts pure...use

God for this. The more you let Him in on your goals, dreams, and hopes, the more work He will be able to do. Remember, we have free will. So we either choose to fill our minds with things of God or things of Satan. We know all those negative doubting thoughts are not of our God!

And the peace of God, which surpasses all understanding, will guard your hearts and your minds in Christ Jesus. Finally, brothers, whatever is true, whatever is honorable, whatever is right, whatever is pure, whatever is lovely, whatever is admirable — if anything is excellent or praiseworthy — think on these things. Whatever you have learned and received and heard from me, and seen in me, put these things into practice. And the God of peace will be with you.... Philippians 4:7-9

EXTERNAL VICTIM: This is a response of passive nature when fear of a result in the outside world holds us back. Rather than risking failure as you grow and pursue your hopes, dreams and passions, you do nothing. You metaphorically "lie in **B.E.D.**" and take on the passive role of victim.

B.E.D.

B=Blame: Too often when we try a new venture and experience, our first setback we throw in the towel, blaming the setback for quitting, like...
- It took much money to invest.
- I don't have the support of my family or friends.
- I am too busy taking care of everyone else- there is no time for me.

E=Excuse: At the risk of trying something new or making mistakes that may cost us financially, emotionally, or just put us in unfamiliar territory, we often make excuses to not even begin the process out of fear of the potential failure.

- *Have I not commanded you? Be strong and courageous. Do not be afraid; do not be discouraged, for the Lord your God will be with you wherever you go."* Joshua 1:9

D=Denial: This tugs at my heart strings more than the rest. You were born valuable enough. God made you and loves you-thus you are enough. But too often, with time in this tainted world, we slowly find ourselves in a place where we truly deny our heart, mind, and soul the opportunity to dream.

- *Therefore we do not lose heart. Though outwardly we are wasting away, yet inwardly we are being renewed day by day. For our light and momentary troubles are achieving for us an eternal glory that far outweighs them all. So we fix our eyes not on what is seen, but on what is unseen, since what is seen is temporary, but what is unseen is eternal.* 2 Corinthians 4:16-18

> **Consider the Problem:** Are we looking to external sources for drive, strength or worthiness?

Dream Big

When we are confident that we have placed God in the center of our dreams, the eternal blessings that this verse speaks of, will bring confidence and support on an overwhelming level of hope. Dreams designed only for worldly gain fall weak, produce shallowly, and will not sustain. Whatever your dream (home, life, work), I want your dreams to be part of Jesus's Legacy. Dreams that bring glory to God, faith to the faint hearted, and life to the dead…these are the dreams that last a life time.

THE WORD

CHAPTER 14
WHAT IF YOU HAD A MAP?

MISTAKES MATTER

MISTAKES MATTER

THE WORD

WHAT IF YOU HAD A MAP?

Do you remember those maze puzzles found in the back of magazines where there are a dozen routes to take but only one leads to the "X"? Consider your life here on earth as a maze. God is up above. He sees your path and all the mistaken paths. He knows how many times it will take you to get to the right one. He knows the effects of your labor, and the trials you will endure. He knows every detail which you cannot know.

If you knew it would take you four tries to get your dream, goal, gift (the "X"), would you stop at three?

What if you had a map that guaranteed your protection and guidance as you set out on this journey? Would you use it?

In Part 4, Mistakes Matter, we use chapter 14, the "Consider the Word" chapter, to remind us that we do have a map to show us the way, and we do have a guide who says He will protect us. We will consider how stepping out in faith, is what's needed for our growth and to prepare us for what lies ahead-even knowing that we may make some mistakes, and trusting that those very mistakes are crucial to our growth.

THE 'WORD' IS OUR MAP

- *Your word is a lamp for my feet, a light on my path.* Psalm 119:105
- *All Scripture is God-breathed and is useful for teaching, rebuking, correcting and training in righteousness, 17 so that the servant of God[a] may be thoroughly equipped for every good work.* 2 Timothy 3:16-17
- *If you remain in me and my words remain in you, ask whatever you wish, and it will be done for you.* John 15:7
- *"Every word of God is flawless; he is a shield to those who take refuge in him.* Proverbs 30:5
- *For the word of the Lord is right and true; he is faithful in all he does.* Psalm 33:4

> **Consider the Word:** The Bible is our map with every bit of instruction one could ask for.

GOD IS OUR GUIDE

- *You make known to me the path of life;* Psalm 16:11
- *My steps are ordered by the Lord.* Psalm 37:23 (ESV)
- *So do not fear, for I am with you; do not be dismayed, for I am your God. I will strengthen you and help you; I will uphold you with my righteous right hand.* Isaiah 41:10
- *He will not let your foot slip—he who watches over you will not slumber;* Psalm 121:3
- *Since you are my rock and my fortress, for Your sake of your lead me and guide me.* Psalm 31:3
- *I will instruct you and teach you in the way you should go; I will counsel you with my loving eye on you.* Psalm 32:8
- *The Lord is my shepherd, I lack nothing.* Psalm 23:1
- *Trust in the Lord with all your heart and lean not on your own understanding; in all your ways submit to him, and he will make your paths straight.* Proverbs 3:5-6

- *This is what the Lord says-your Redeemer, the Holy One of Israel: "I am the Lord your God, who teaches you what is best for you, who directs you in the way you should go.* Isaiah 48:17

This chapter can be a little misleading, and I want to take a minute to be sure and impress upon each reader that this is not a chapter exclusively for those desiring to go out on a new path, or just for those called to sell all their personal possessions and hit the road!

Jesus has called for us all and for some, it's in their current place!

If I could do anything, it would be to inspire others to dream a God dream, labor in God's plan specifically designed for them, see life and others with our Father's Eyes, listen to the Holy Spirit our friend, and to accept the abundant life only Christ can offer.

Whether simply witnessing right in your current place, or by living out a beautiful Godly marriage, or raising wise and talented children of God, or serving beyond the call of duty.... NEVER doubt your place as long as you feel you are working for the Lord and this work sits right with your soul.

- Pray for insight and to know what God wants of you and your place here.
- Trust in God's strength, support, and love as you pursue your purpose.
- Give praises along the way to your maker, who made you just the way you are, perfectly imperfect to do His great work, not your own.

"One of the greatest ways to disciple to others is to simply live what we say we believe."

Consider the word: Jesus commanded <u>us all</u> to go and make disciples. To teach others the Biblical principles He taught his disciples. To live a life that draws others to Him and also to share our faith.

This is why we ALL need "Faith Infused Living" back into our daily lives...God wants us to have insight and understanding of His teaching. This helps us to be passionate in our faith, to be contagious as we live, to be ready and present as doors open to us. This is why it is so important to keep in the habit of meeting, so instruction falls on ready hearts and fertilized soil.

I will counsel you with my loving eye on you. Do not be like the horse or the mule, which have no understanding but must be controlled by bit and bridle or they will not come to you. Psalm 32:8-9

Our calling may be in a new job, as a parent, a CEO, a business owner, a teacher, hair stylist, CPA, CNA... still you have been called. Each of us in various ways, but all for the good work of our Lord.

I do not want one person to let fear of making mistakes hold them back from going deep or venturing out... but rather to trust in the Lord to build them up!

THE GIFT

CHAPTER 15

WHAT IF THE PRIZE IS BEYOND YOUR IMAGINATION?

MISTAKES MATTER

MISTAKES MATTER

THE GIFT

WHAT IF THE PRIZE IS BEYOND YOUR IMAGINATION?

We've already established that when making a life goal, when trying to follow your calling, or when going after your dreams, you need to be in line with God's teachings and desires. Believe it or not, this is only half the battle. If we are real with ourselves, a lot of us have hang-ups about success, being blessed greatly, or possessing what we might consider too much.

This is a tricky topic for me, and I believe Christians everywhere. Are we supposed to hope for prosperity, and look to the prize? I say, *not exactly.* I do think we need to understand God's desire for us and just how He desires to "**grace** us with it." Check out these two verses.

> *Keep this Book of the Law always on your lips; meditate on it day and night, so that you may be careful to do everything written in it. Then you will be prosperous and successful.* Joshua 1:8

> *The thief comes only to steal and kill and destroy; I have come that they may have life, and have it to the full.* John 10:10

Think about how these two verses affirm what we have been talking about. First, we've learned that it is crucial to have the 'Word' and God working in our lives, goals, and dreams. And, if we want the abundance spoken of in these verses, it is required. Second, in John 10:10 Jesus is speaking, which affirms it is **by the grace of Jesus that we are able to even receive this abundance.**

What a relief! What human could do what is written in Joshua 1:8, (meditate day and night and do everything that is written). But we have a Savior... not to abuse, but to use. Without our Savior, true prosperity and success spoken in this verse would be unattainable.

We can't just read the 'Word' and 'clock-in' at church. We need to have **hearts that desire to keep the Book of the Law always on our lips, hearts that desire to meditate on it day and night, and hearts that carefully try to carry out what is written.** This is much of Fulfill Your Legacy's philosophy. I feel passionate about finding ways to infuse faith, the Word, and God into our days.

Christ Blesses Us & Then What?

The more people that God puts me in contact with, the more accountable I feel for carrying out more of His work, and for doing it better with each day. Abundance of all kinds is bestowed and here I am talking about receiving more clients. So, if you receive spiritual gifts, worldly talent, financial gain, or both, you are then more accountable for these blessings.

> **Consider the Gift:** What if the gift seems too big for us? Or that we are not worthy; or that others may feel we are not worthy? I ask you then, is this blessing just for you to greedily blow or are you using your gift wisely?

The thing is, it isn't always easy using blessings wisely. One way to help us do this is by remembering **these blessings are not OUR windfalls.** Surely we have all witnessed or been a part of the destruction that can come from money or material abundance used unwisely. I have to believe it's terribly heartbreaking for our Father to watch us use what He meant for good as a tool for crafting destruction.

Something I want to stress is how abundance should not be confused with money alone. All of God's blessings can be given unto us. If we shy away from material blessings... does an abundance of kind heartedness or compassion seem more noble then? I dare say "no." It has all to do with what we do with the blessing. It's nothing short of horrible when either gift is not shared and used for the glory of God. Both are noble, when shared and used in the glory of God. (Reread the "Parable of the Talents," Matthew 25:14–30)

But it's my blessing, can't I use it how I please?

Absolutely! When we truly commit our work as work of the Lord, we then understand that the blessings received of it are not ours either. This is why I put so much effort into pushing us to work as working for the Lord, for His purpose, with all that He can offer us, as we carry out our days.

Sure, we can simply do our job, and do it well. Yes, we can get worldly rewards from it. Then 'yes,' go ahead and use it as you please. In fact, you will feel compelled to do just that! It is natural, and human, and fine. Even if you abide by reputable worldly laws, you may get some real enjoyment out of that reward. **But, I want more for you. And so does God!**

When we really do as written, when we are living examples of Christ carrying out our days to the best of our ability, we WANT to work as working for the Lord. We then KNOW the results of this labor are not our own. It is an overwhelming sense of gratitude we feel for these blessings of God. This overwhelming understanding walks along with us as we are then compelled to do just as the Word says–use those blessings in turn, wisely again, and so it goes.

If this sounds a little odd to you, then I challenge you. Because let me tell you, if you have enjoyed the rewards of hard labor that YOU alone have done up to this point...**just wait until you put your energy and purpose into carrying out your work FOR the Lord!**

Wait until you reap the blessings of your labor for the Lord. Wait until you have God's blessing in your hands and really understand that it isn't yours alone.

I can best describe this in terms of dependence or freedom. Working on your own terms with your own energy and waiting on the worldly gain is very dependent. Dependent on whom? Flesh and the world, your flesh, your boss, your energy, your customers, the market? Think of the folks that have been ripped off by the workforce? Did they not work hard? Most did. This can be a pretty horrible feeling, to be at the mercy of this world.

When truly working for the Lord and submitting yourself, your labor, and your life to Him, He is completely behind you. He is your strength, He is aligning new paths, opening new doors, giving you blessings. If you were going to slide over and let anyone take the wheel, so to speak, can you imagine how much better your life would be if it were the Lord, versus the world, that you let navigate your life? When you give yourself to the Lord, give your marriage, your parenting, your job, and more to the Lord, you have freedom to gain things above the world; you are not limited by the world!

Consider the Gift: Joy, hope, peace, love, and contentment even amidst afflictions.

Be joyful in hope, patient in affliction, faithful in prayer. Romans 12:12

So what about when things go badly while working for the Lord? How do you explain that then?

This is another good question we can consider. When things go badly, and they will in this world, we need to remember that we are living in the flesh here and in a sinful world. Sometimes no matter how hard we try, we get mixed up in the paths of all kinds of bad. But, when things go badly, who do you want to be dependent on? Dependent on the world and all of its limits? How well do you think you will handle set-backs when you have taught yourself to DEPEND on things of the world, a world that Satan loves to tear us apart in.

Now what if you had worked for the Lord and there was adversity within your work, home, or life? Does submitting or 'giving' yourself to God and all His power, strength, insight and protection sound a bit better? Because when you submit your life and work to God, it does mean you get all those blessings among your trials; God's power, strength, insight, and protection.

Better yet, remember the cause and effect I spoke of in 'Making Wise Choices'? The worldly effect of trials, when solely depending on the world, results in a lot of turmoil as we trudge through hardship.

With the Lord, when we stay close to Him under hardship, we cannot forget what happens.... He blesses us for being faithful with a straightened path and more character! This only affirms to us His glory and the power of Jesus Christ in our lives.

> **Consider the Gift:** Jesus Christ our Savior, who offers us a life of freedom from this world, and the control over Satan's destruction.

"...In this you rejoice, though now for a little while, if necessary, you have been grieved by various trials, so that the tested genuineness of your faith—more precious than gold that perishes though it is tested by fire—may be found

to result in praise and glory and honor at the revelation of Jesus Christ." 1 Peter 1:6-7

Which sounds better, the freedom of just working hard, as working for the glory of the Lord, and letting Him work out the details, mapping your steps, being there to catch you, OR, working for the world and being dependent on the world and at the mercy of Satan?

If there is one thing for you to try after reading this book, I would suggest it be this-commit to work for the Lord! Some of you do this and absolutely know what I mean. You are shaking your head back and forth with an affirming nod, and agreeing with me with a finger pointed up to the heavens. If not, IT'S OKAY-we are all at different places. But, the one gift I do not want you missing out on is... **The FREEDOM found in Christ-filled living!**

All blessings bestowed upon us need to be handled with great wisdom and grace.

By staying in the 'Word' we gain insight. As God dwells in us, we gain wisdom, and as we accept Christ as our savior, we are graced, and therefore give grace. We can be gifted with all kinds of blessings. We need to WAKE UP to them, acknowledge them for what they are, master them, use them wisely, and be ready for more.

On December 23, 2015, I had a blog posting on this very matter. I had just finished working with a client who painstakingly admitted that she quite possibly had held herself back from what she truly thought would be a lucrative business that would use her talent and help others. She was already a very successful woman in her currently-owned business. She had pretty much laid out the whole plan to me saying she had dreamt of doing this for years.

We had built a lot of trust in our coaching by this time. **She had deepened her faith tremendously over the months, which is part of why she was even aware of this dream being held** captive. **More importantly, she now recognized a growing passion pulling her to help these individuals dear to her heart.**

We had just spent hours brainstorming her strategy for success and how she planned to use the inevitable blessings that would follow. We discussed giving back financially to those in need, in proportion, and how much more she would gain with this new venture. We worked and worked on what was holding her back and finally she had a break through. **She very humbly admitted that she had not moved forward due to her fear about others judging her, or fearing that they may think she was not worthy.**

I simply made one statement and asked one question.

"I can understand wondering what others might think of your success if you go ahead with this."

"I wonder what God will think **if you don't?**"

With realism and humility, she stared at me for a second, nodded and said, **"Let's get busy serving the Lord!"**

Consider the Gift:
- Insight and clarity that will see past Satan's lies
- Strength and power to do what you once thought impossible

Clarity ~ Priceless

Clarity is a gift given when you are faith infused, when the Word is presently in your heart, when God is actively living in you and you in Him, when the awareness of Jesus dying on the cross for YOUR very sins is embedded within you. You have insight, strength and power to do great things in the Lord's name!

As I have been writing this book, I find myself amazed in how God has been moving in me far before I even thought about a book. I have been shocked from the day I started my coaching certification at the way my plans, programs, connections, and even teachings have all blended together with perfect timing. I could not have known the way my company name would fit into my book, how my passion would lead me on the faith-filled journey, and even how some blog postings, with time, would show insight into things I barely grasped when I wrote them. I decided to write this book in April of 2016. Here is my December, 2015 blog...

> **Consider the Gift:** He is working when we aren't even aware of it.
>
> This clarity often hits us after the fact, but it is still Him who worked in us all along. We need to be aware of this and give Him due credit or we may miss an opportunity to let more of His power work in us.

December, 23rd 2015, Fulfill Your Legacy Blog Posting on Awaking.

But it is the spirit in a person, the breath of the Almighty, that gives them understanding. Job 32:8

I am always fascinated by the reforming God does in us...How the Holy Spirit stirs in us...and, gives us deeper insight. I love how we grow, how at times I look back at things I once thought right, but now, like a parent, I feel loving humility at my own immaturity. How amazing God is to lovingly watch us grow. Allow us to grow. We have free will and we know letting God and the Holy Spirit come dwell in us will give us the insight we need to become the most Christ-like version of ourselves.

- Breathe God into your heart, soul and mind!
- Ask for the Holy Spirit to dwell in you more today than yesterday and let that insight take root.
- Watch yourself be who God wants you to be.

As we let more God in...we let more love in.
Love is gracious and kind, selfless and patient...these
are the days I want to awake to ~Niccie Kliegl, CLC

> **Consider the Gift:** Increased insight, blessings of all kinds, and the responsibility to do and give more.

We really do not need to worry about where we are starting at in any given plan. We know that with God and the Holy Spirit on our side, we will be growing. They will be leading us, arranging our steps, giving us strength; and before we know it, their insight will be right in front of us-having brought us through the rough spots and up to a new level of understanding and fulfillment.

"Mistakes teach us & take us to a new level."

In Chapter 14 I made reference to us needing a map and how much easier it would be to make our way to our destination if we had one. I also used an analogy with the use of a maze to encourage you to keep trying for your dreams. I explained how there may be four routes one can take, with three being dead ends, but one route reaches the final destination-the prize.

I use this metaphor while coaching too, because I really like for my clients to consider each failed attempt an opportunity to be that much closer to 'perfect,' their 'right' path.

In healthcare especially, I have always welcomed a "near miss." These are occurrences that cause no harm but clue you in on an area that could have been bad. This will be an area to fix before there is a bad result. (For instance, an Alzheimer's unit may have a code to enter and exit that alarms if the door is used without punching in the code-a safety measure to then go check if a confused patient left without assistance. A nurse witnesses a visitor use the door and the alarm sounded quieter than usual. She takes measures to report this and have it fixed before the alarm could completely disable or silence allowing a patient to leave without anyone knowing).

One hates to think of how even the smallest things do or could result in major consequences but these errors or near misses are opportunities to be even better tomorrow.

> **Consider the Gift:** Near misses.
>
> When God is on our side, I believe He offers us near misses. He carefully watches over us and helps us get through some pretty scary situations unscathed. We need to be wise to this. It will help build trust and faith in our partnership and relationship with God.

If we are really living our true purpose… shouldn't things come easily? Yes, and no, doors will open. God will direct our steps, He will even straighten our paths and keep us from harm. But…

He will NOT keep us from growing!

If He knows we CAN DO MORE, He will refine and perfect us! This is a good thing–be humble and take it! This growth will later become one of your greatest blessings!

I know God gives us what we can handle with a goal of refining us. One of the most difficult deeds for me with this line of work is my writing. Not the ideas, concepts or ability to express myself…but the grammar, spelling, and sentence structure.

I am not real sure what I thought I would be doing, but I absolutely had no idea I would be writing daily blogs and becoming an author. God has mysterious ways of working. I'd have probably run for cover if I had known just what I was getting into. But I heard God calling me, and I went.

He is working on me constantly-**just as He is working on you.** What do you suppose God is hoping you will grow through?

The hopes and dreams I find myself helping others through are so varied-building a Godly marriage, parenting that builds up and partners with God, regaining physical health, moving up at work, navigating through a transition like a new job, loss of a spouse, or divorce, or even stepping out on a totally new venture. It really works the same for us all when we choose to join up with God.

He knows what He is doing for you and for me...just like my client who decided to step out in faith to start her own company.

"Let's get busy serving the Lord!"

Therefore, I urge you, brothers and sisters, in view of God's mercy, to offer your bodies as a living sacrifice, holy and pleasing to God—this is your true and proper worship. Do not conform to the pattern of this world, but be transformed by the renewing of your mind. Then you will be able to test and approve what God's will is—his good, pleasing and perfect will. Romans 12:1-2

THE CHOICE

CHAPTER 16
WHAT IF GOD WAS ON YOUR SIDE, WHAT IF HE WASN'T?

MISTAKES MATTER

MISTAKES MATTER

THE CHOICE

WHAT IF GOD WAS ON YOUR SIDE, WHAT IF HE WASN'T?

"Whoever is not with me is against me, and whoever does not gather with me scatters. Matthew 12:30

The Word clearly tells you we are either with Him or against Him. I expect by now you are feeling pretty rooted in the Word and the Triune God. But, you can still find yourselves stuck with fear at times. Fear of making mistakes is often what keeps us from trying new things, from growing.

Fear can be so crippling. But, beware!
I want you to think real hard on who you are fearing.

The only fear you should let sink into your soul is fear of the Almighty Father, who is on your side and has loads of power. Power that can take you far beyond your dreams. God's power is in, of, and above this world. Chapter 16 transforms your position on growth to no longer let the fear of failure, darkness, or turmoil hold you back from the future God has intended for you!

I will touch on two key points in this chapter. First, we will get straight in our minds who we will serve (the Lord or the devil-yep, it is that black and white) ...that shouldn't take but a minute. Then, we will go deeply into how this looks in your life.

Why consider who we're serving & who we're fearing?

It's clear that not one of us wants to serve the devil, and I actually don't even like speaking or typing the name. However, we need to be wise to his power and his desires to keep us from doing God's work. Please see the verses below to be wise to the wolf. He is prowling around waiting to snatch or scatter us.

- This is how the devil tries to get us.
  - » Tempts us with sins of the flesh (glutton, lust...)
  - » Tempts with sins of heart and mind (jealousy, anger, doubt...)
  - » Tries to convince us God doesn't care
- What can you do about it?
  - » *"Put on the full armor of God so that you can take your stand against the devil's schemes"* (Ephesians 6:11).
    - **Belt:** Stand firm then, with the belt of truth buckled around your waist
    - **Breastplate:** of righteousness in place
    - **Boots:** feet fitted with the readiness that comes from the gospel of peace.
    - **Shield:** of faith, with which you can extinguish all the flaming arrows of the evil one.
    - **Helmet:** of salvation and the sword of the Spirit, which is the word of God.
  - » Educate yourself so you see the devil's deceitful ways and you can give them no heed. (Some helpful insights found below.)
  - » *"Submit yourselves, then, to God. Resist the devil, and he will flee from you"* James 4:7
  - » When we become Christians we are no longer citizens of the world-we are God's and God is ours. Being of the world is scary...that is where the devil can rule.

> **Consider the Choice:** Fear of the god of the world. Or fear of the Almighty GOD of love? By choosing you let one reign in your life.

Two Thoughts On Fearing Evil!

1. So often I hear people disappointed in themselves for falling short or prey to sin of this kind, claiming that they must have let the devil tempt them or that they were bad or feel like a weak Christian.

I acknowledge that by all means. And, I love the diligent heart of these folks. However, *they then let 'dark' win twice.* My suggestion is that the second they ALLOW themselves to recognize a sinful nature, they quickly shoot God a prayer that thanks Him for the blessing of clarity they possess for being wise to it!

Think of all the individuals stuck in the foothold of sin, unable to see goodness or recognize sin at all. My heart weeps for them.

As a Christian, Satan will not be able to RULE over you (you are free from sin and not a slave to sin- with Christ). That is what the Word says! However, it doesn't mean that Satan won't try. It also doesn't disregard the fact that you are living here in the flesh.

"The key is filling up with so much good that the devil can't stand to be around you-or any of your friends or loved ones...thinking you all are a lost cause!"

Never give the devil another opportunity to delight. Rather, use your insight from falling short as a way to send HIM off fleeing, as he quickly realizes he has no dominion over you. You are God's and your mishaps are overseen by the Lord, who is making each one into a stepping stone to God's greatness.

2. The devil will not waste his time on someone of no value to him. So if you are in a place of upcoming growth and development or prosperity among Godliness, then he may try one quick attack, knowing just how much power you will soon have in the name of the Lord. Do NOT be thrown off by this…. recognize it and shout praises to your Father as you are near a break through and safely tucked within the protection of the Almighty.

There is a legend or parable that I cannot find the original creator of, but I still want to share it with you. This story is about two great wolves, both strong and powerful. One is white and represents all things good in us, the other is black representing our bad. They do not coexist so when they meet, they fight until one wins and one leaves. Which do you suppose wins?

The one we feed…

> **Consider the Choice:** Recognize when the devil is up to his antics or fall prey to his works like bad dreams, shouts of insecurities, things constantly breaking or even health scares….
>
> Or, call on the Almighty who can send the devil running for cover!

Two Thoughts On Fearing God!

We will break this down into two parts again. First, looking at what it means to fear God, and then looking at how after we CHOOSE God, He can help us grow through our mistakes and apprehension.

1. So what do you mean-to fear God?

This one used to really bother me. How could I fear God? I just couldn't get it. I had met God and even as I saw my sins before Him I did not fear Him-he still loved me. I hated to think really intelligent theologians possibly had this all wrong. ☺ But, the truth is, I get it now.

The best way I can explain fearing God is as an awe and understanding of the immense power, knowledge, and control He has. We of course love that He has all this power and control, but we are not seeing the big picture if we forget what all that power can do.

*As a Christian I suggest not fearing this power in terms of it being used **against you** (fearing God's power as a non-believer is all together different). For believers the power He has may be used **for you**.*

I touched on this in Chapter 1, and I do see the magnitude of giving complete submission to God (You are His) and then fearing just what He may ask of you. My advice is to humbly pray.

2. So we have CHOSEN to be WITH God and now what?

Once we partner with God, the abundance comes. Even while learning you will need to be prepared for more growing, but it does NOT mean you will be without heartache, pain, or trials. Rest assured... goodness awaits!

Sometimes people feel no need to progress or strive for more...that they have learned to be content where they are at in life. (I fear they consider this concept only in relation to material possessions, Godly supply, and so on). I love this content lifestyle so much! I also understand how giving yourself up to God, truly putting your trust in Him and His plans for you, whether in plenty or want, is so freeing and right.

There is great honor in learning how to be content with what you have and where you are at in life. That, however, has more to do with 'not wanting.'

'Not growing' is something altogether different!

"Enlarge the place of your tent; Stretch out the curtains of your dwellings, spare not; Lengthen your cords and strengthen your pegs... as in Isaiah 54:2

I love Isaiah 54:2 on enlarging your space. I think of my heart and body as my tent and curtains. As the verse says, open your curtains and let new light in. I hear, open your home and self, to offer goodness and shelter to others.

- Lengthen your cord and tighten your pegs? Indeed, a tent cannot expand with the same limits binding it in place. Thus, I challenge us with...
- Allow your boundaries to expand.
- Allow God's light to shine in and give you insight and strength to do and grow.
- Keep your peg or foundation firmly within Christ's love and God's teaching as you
  - fear not in this newly found place,
  - but rather in the ability of your father to get you there!

Consider the Choice: Locking our mistakes up from ourselves and from God...giving us no room for growth...robbing God the opportunity to refine us and to use us in a more perfect way to do His work...or stretching ourselves, partnering with God and submitting to His plans.

PART 5
FORGIVENESS
FULFILLS

THE PROBLEM

CHAPTER 17

YOU DO NEED TO RECOGNIZE WHAT LACK OF FORGIVENESS IS DOING TO YOUR LIFE

FORGIVENESS FULFILLS

Forgiveness Fulfills

THE PROBLEM

YOU DO NEED TO RECOGNIZE WHAT LACK OF FORGIVENESS IS DOING TO YOUR LIFE

Why is forgiveness so hard? Possibly because it wipes out all control we have over a situation. The truth is we have no control over another individual's actions, and we surely cannot make others say they are sorry just because we want to hear it. If not having control isn't bad enough, waiting on others to say they are sorry adds fuel to the fire, because this now lets the other person actually gain control OVER us. By us not forgiving one another, we let the effects of being unforgiven have a foothold on both parties involved.

What does staying in the place of unforgiving
do to our mind and spirit?

- Look at these concepts from Matthew 6:21, *For where your treasure is, there your heart will be also...*

- and from Proverbs 23:7, *For as he thinketh in his heart, so is he......*

Not forgiving with the mind, creates illness in our heart (emotionally) AND body (physically).

Emotional & Physical Affects of Not Forgiving	
Emotional	Physical
Increase susceptibility to addictions, drugs & alcohol	Increased head/neck tension... leading to headaches
Low Self Esteem	Stomachaches
Deprives self of opportunities	Dizziness
Push through harmful relationships	Fatigue
Push through poor work settings	Digestion difficulties
Depression	Teeth grinding
Increased agitation	Constricted blood flow to the heart
Health & Wellness, The Emotional and Physical Effects of Not Forgiving, Rich Cavaness, May 2013	

So how do we get free of these footholds?

Let's use Jesus as our example. After we let Jesus take our sins, we are freed of them, and those sins no longer have a foothold on us. Likewise, when we forgive others, we are also freed-freed from the negative effects of holding onto that foothold.

It wasn't until I started coaching people on forgiveness that I really started to see forgiveness for the two-part process it is.

- Letting go of any position over the other person...It is God's job to work on them.
- Taking care of self...God wants you healthy and strong, growing and loving, NOT stuck in a foothold hindering yourself from so much joy.

True life story of a beautiful Christian woman caught in two footholds & freed from both

Here is her story:

This story began when I was a young girl of six. People saw me as a sweet little girl who came from a family who loved me very deeply. My parents divorced and my siblings and I remained in our mother's home with visits every other weekend to our father's. It all seemed pretty amicable to me when looking back, but there was a twinge of something missing or lacking about it all.

I had my first date at 16, only to find myself in a possessive relationship which quickly grew out of control. The school, the church, and my family were all very supportive, but at such a young age, I was left very confused about love, comfort, and acceptance. With everyone's help I was able to break free from this emotionally abusive relationship, but it was all very surreal.

I dated very little after that, only to find myself pregnant and in what I thought was love at age eighteen. I married this man, and our relationship, too, was difficult. I worked very hard on this marriage and spent ten years with many ups and downs, until eventually I found myself in a situation where I had to face my husband's infidelity. This left me feeling emotionally unloved and insecure. This relationship eventually ended as well.

On the immediate rebound of this so-called failure, as I saw it, I found myself quickly recognizing a man's attention and possession as love and affection. This was the worst relationship thus far. Again, for ten years I pushed through this relationship trying to make it work. I regularly went to church with my children finding church and work my only solace.

This man I married chose not to grow with me, but rather wanted to take me down with him. He became an alcoholic not too long into the marriage, battling with his own mental illnesses that he took out on himself and our family. He had addictions to gambling and sex as well, which began to poison my life, and the lives of our children. I slowly began to lose the person I used to be, until I realized one day that I was looking in the mirror at a stranger. It was at this point that I knew I had to get away!

This time, however, I went straight to the ONE who would fix it all. The ONE I could always trust and depend on. The ONE who would teach me the value I possessed and the honor I needed to uphold myself to…for no other reason than because **I was his and he was mine***.*

SHE was HIS & HE was Hers

She spent 6 years learning how to forgive herself and others, how to heal herself, and how to become in and of God. Not too long ago she was reflecting back on her changes. She remembered the day she moved on and went to God in her Father's house, immediately feeling a release of weight-heaviness that for years was making her sick. She remembered how even years after she was freed from all this abuse, control, and fear, that she would look back with unease.

But with time, and a growing relationship with God, her Father, without even being aware of it until it was upon her, she found herself looking back at images of those times. Seeing old picture albums and recalling the times of past, she no longer associated them with negative emotions.

The pictures were now void of their original pain and loss. How could this be? She seemed surprised, and yet, even speaking it out loud, she knew how…

God, the Almighty, of all things good dwelled in her.

Where He is, evil is not.

No, those horrible years are not removed from her past, but the pain, heartache, embarrassment, insecurity, shame, and all things that do not come from God, left her as she learned to TRULY LEAVE IT ALL AT THE CROSS!

This story is like many where we find ourselves stuck in a past hurt, and it simply carries us to the next. If we don't resolve past hurts by really getting to the bottom of them, where the real healing and forgiveness comes, all we are doing is running from them. The devil will use that place of pain and hurt to get a foothold on us, if we let him. This woman not only spent 6 years learning how to forgive over 20 years of painful male-female relationships and several years of father-child relationship changes, she also learned to forgive herself and all the footholds attached to herself as well. **God is GOOD!**

THE WORD

CHAPTER 18

YOU DO NOT NEED SOMEONE TO SAY SORRY TO YOU FIRST

FORGIVENESS FULFILLS

FORGIVENESS FULFILLS

THE WORD

YOU DO NOT NEED SOMEONE TO SAY SORRY TO YOU FIRST

We pray right out of the Word, "forgive us of our sins as we forgive those who sin against us."
Think on this:

"Forgive us…as we forgive those…," God did not put the request and the command together by accident.

You DO NOT need someone to say sorry to you first. 'Forgiveness' is not responsible for the other person, their behaviors, and their place in life. *Forgiveness is about you letting go of their trespass*, their sin, just as Jesus did for you. Why would you want to hold onto that? You don't!

By not forgiving we are holding on to the past. I want us to look at what lies ahead.

Brothers and sisters, I do not consider myself yet to have taken hold of it. But one thing I do: Forgetting

what is behind and straining toward what is ahead,
Philippians 3:13

Consider the Word: We are instructed to look forward to what lies ahead. Can you image how much grief we could save ourselves if we got good at this?

When we find ourselves thinking, dwelling, or getting stuck in the past, it's often because we've let something that's bothered us from the past, stay alive. To do as Philippians 3:13 says, "... to forget what was behind..." we sometimes need to resolve it first. Dwelling on it, is not resolving.

Some Biblical truth on how to forgive and resolve...

During the 'Consider the Word' Chapter on forgiveness, I researched all kinds of verses on forgiveness, and many related to us letting go and giving up any negative effects left in the wake of a past hurt. I wanted to pull together a nice 'How-to' on forgiveness.

No surprise here. After hours in books and on the internet, Joyce Meyer, and her no-nonsense approach, had just what I was looking for. It simply isn't worth tweaking or writing something original when she had just what I was looking for. (Taken from Joyce's book, *Do Yourself a Favor... Forgive*, Apr 3, 2012.) Here is her...

"3-Part Instructions on How To Forgive"

1. Decide – You will never forgive if you wait until you feel like it. Choose to obey God and steadfastly resist the devil in his attempts to poison you with bitter thoughts. Make a quality decision to forgive, and God will heal your wounded emotions in due time (see **Matthew 6:12-14**).

2. Depend – You cannot forgive without the power of the Holy Spirit. It's too hard to do on your own. If you are truly willing, God will enable you, but you must humble yourself and cry out to Him for help. In **John 20:22-23** Jesus breathed on the disciples and said, «*Receive the Holy Spirit!*» His next instruction was about forgiving people. Ask God to breathe the Holy Spirit on you, so you can forgive those who've hurt you.

3. Obey – The Word tells us several things we're to do concerning forgiving our enemies:

    a. Pray for your enemies and those who abuse and misuse you. Pray for their happiness and welfare (see **Luke 6:27-28**). As you pray, God can give them revelation that will bring them out of deception. They may not even be aware they hurt you, or maybe they're aware but are so self-centered that they don't care. Either way, they need revelation.

    b. ...*Bless and do not curse them* (**Romans 12:14**). In the Greek *to bless* means «to speak well of» and *to curse* means «to speak evil of.» You can't walk in forgiveness *and* be a gossip. You must stop repeating the offense. You can't get over it if you continue to talk about it. **Proverbs 17:9** says that he who covers an offense seeks love.

How Do We Recognize If We've Truly Forgiven

Have you ever had it where you thought you truly gave some past hurt up to Christ, only to have it rear its ugly head again? Well, this isn't uncommon, and I wanted to do a little fact finding with you, which I received out of my certified coaching training. My hope is that it helps to call your attention to any forgiveness falsehoods.

1. "The fear of never moving past this hurt has scared me straight."
   - Forgiveness Falsehood: Being scared straight can work for a period in the flesh. This would be like forcing yourself to greet, do business with, or to interact with someone who has greatly hurt you. With loads of discipline

day after day you can change a pattern of behavior but the energy used to keep this discipline going is draining. True forgiveness is a matter of the heart, done by the love of the LORD, who does not need more love to insure it maintains. Once you forgive another the way Jesus has forgiven you, it is done. No more energy is needed. All that is left is health-a healed relationship on your side.

2. "He said he was sorry and bought me flowers two days in a row, so I know he is sorry."
   • Forgiveness Falsehood: A short-term display of changed behavior is no indication that you, who is performing the behavior, is truly sorry or has been forgiven... or that the other person, by performing kind behaviors, is in fact truly sorry or forgiven. True forgiveness is unconditional.

3. "I don't understand how I no longer feel resentment."
   • Forgiveness Fact: One truly is able to remove the negative effects from a past hurt through the help of Christ. Forgiveness Falsehoods involve the person still living in that past hurt, which keeps pain and hurt alive.

4. "I keep having to forgive her. I absolutely forgave her when she did it, but I just keep coming back to what she did, and then I need to forgive her again." Forgiveness Falsehood, I had to say this because I don't want to admit this catches me up sometimes...but it's true. We simply didn't give it all up! Ugh! So giddy-up and try harder, put a little more heart into it, or pray for more hope and healing. If your heart is in it, don't worry-It will happen when it should. And remember how valuable it is that you can give it up day after day until it is gone for good...this will help keep the devil's hands out of your life while your working it out.

Therefore, as God's chosen people, holy and dearly loved, clothe yourselves with compassion, kindness, humility, gentleness, and patience. Bear with each other and forgive one another if any of you has a grievance against someone. Forgive as the Lord forgave you. And over all these virtues put on love, which binds them all together in perfect unity.
Colossians 3:12-14

Consider the Word: Sin alienates us from God and gives Satan a role in our lives. Whether it is our sin or another's that we are carrying around in our heart, it is shutting out God's work. Let's do like the Word says and forgive them of their sins as we have been forgiven, so we can move on from them. No more will they dwell in us, keeping us from a deeper relationship with our Father, His work, and love.

It is what Christ died for and what God wants of us!

For I will forgive their wickedness and will remember their sins no more." Hebrews 8:12

THE GIFT

CHAPTER 19

YOU DO NOT NEED TO USE THE TOOLS YOU'VE BEEN GIVEN

FORGIVENESS FULFILLS

FORGIVENESS FULFILLS

THE GIFT

YOU DO NOT NEED TO USE THE TOOLS YOU'VE BEEN GIVEN

Forgiveness does not excuse the other person's behavior. Forgiveness prevents their behavior from destroying your heart. ~ Unknown

If you feel you don't have it in you to forgive, you probably don't. Sorry, but it's okay! You'd be Christ if you were perfect! God, Jesus, and the Holy Spirit have it in them, and they are in you!

This chapter is all about the gift we have in using God, Jesus, and the Holy Spirit. I really think it can sometimes be just too hard for these sinful bodies to forgive big hurts. But, that doesn't mean we live in them, or that we let them live in us. When we let past hurts dwell in us, it simply takes up the room God wants to do His living in each and every one of us!

We can't forget our free will here on earth. All these gifts from God are here for all of us. But, the choice to use them and live in them is always ours. Chapter 19 is devoted to the gift we have and can call on for help when we simply can't forgive on our own.

> **Consider the gift:** Followers of Christ-all we need to do is ask.

We need to ask for help forgiving ourselves or others!

You desire and do not have, so you murder. You covet and cannot obtain, so you fight and quarrel. You do not have, because you do not ask. James 4:2

Ask ~ Seek ~ Knock

"Ask, and it will be given to you; seek, and you will find; knock, and it will be opened to you. "For everyone who asks receives, and he who seeks finds, and to him who knocks it will be opened. Matthew 7:7-8

ASK (Pray to God continually)
Do not be anxious about anything, but in every situation, by prayer and petition, with thanksgiving, present your requests to God. Philippians 4:6

- Think about how likely Satan will be lingering around if all you're doing is talking to God.
- This is conversational, something you do with someone you are in a relationship with. Don't worry, He is capable of hearing and being engaged with us all. Don't ask how, He just is!
- This keeps you in a good and right place day and night.
- Ask & WAIT. This is the hard part. But God tells us he has good things in store for us, and we have faith in Him, so we must ask and wait, ask and wait, ask and

wait. He will answer. It is not always with a response we expected, but He will always answer, and it will always be loving.

- Make your request clear.

SEEK (With all of your heart)

For I know the plans I have for you," declares the Lord, "plans to prosper you and not to harm you, plans to give you hope and a future. Then you will call on me and come and pray to me, and I will listen to you. You will seek me and find me when you seek me with all your heart. Jeremiah 29:11-13

- I like this. With all your heart…that means you care, you believe!
- Before I found myself working hard at joining up with God, and when we were raising our little girls, we had an incident of swearing where I quickly learned to shape up my language. But, the story fits here perfectly. Both Jeff and I come from families that worked hard. We never did a job half way and taught the girls the same. Regardless, at Riley's first grade conference her teacher kindly had a few things around the room to show us. She leads us to the wall with a snicker under her breath. Things About Our Family… 1) I have a mom, dad and sister 2) We don't do things *half fast* at our house…. Well, from then on we both shaped up our language. The lesson behind this story stays the same, whether relating to a prayer or a job done well, whatever you do, do it with everything you've got. **Don't do a half-way prayer!**

(We can see it, to seek it)
The god of this age has blinded the minds of unbelievers, so that they cannot see the light of the gospel that displays the glory of Christ, who is the image of God. 2 Corinthians 4: 4

- With Christ we can see what to seek. My heart breaks for the non believers who have the god of the world blinding them. Let's do what we can to plant a seed in them. Let them see the light!

KNOCK (To inquire, always wanting more)
To be made new in the attitude of your minds; and to put on the new self, created to be like God in true righteousness and holiness. Ephesians 4: 23-24

- This is just how it works. Once you let the light in, the mold can't grow.
- We became renewed each time we adopt a new insight. This leads us to more, which enables us to be more, learn more, and desire more good. This cycle goes on and on.
- God wants you to keep knocking.

You, Lord, are forgiving and good, abounding in love to all who call to you. Psalms 86:5

Consider the gift: God, Jesus and the Holy Spirit!... are we using them?

THE CHOICE

CHAPTER 20

YOU DON'T HAVE TO FORGIVE, YOU DO HAVE A CHOICE

FORGIVENESS FULFILLS

FORGIVENESS FULFILLS

THE CHOICE

YOU DON'T HAVE TO FORGIVE, YOU DO HAVE A CHOICE

"Forgiveness is the fragrance that the violet sheds on the heel that has crushed it." –Mark Twain.

Part 5's 'Consider Your Choice' chapter, takes forgiveness to another level. "Forgive for their sake!" By now the cycle of Consider Your Problem, Consider the Word, Consider the Gift, and Consider the Choice are becoming routine.

Thus far, Part 5 has focused on forgiving to help **you** evolve, to keep you close to God and living with Him. This is crucial. However, **Jesus forgave us because He loved us. "For our sake."** Even though we hurt Him, mocked Him, and betrayed Him, He loved us and forgave us! Forgiving, for no other reason than love, is a far greater gift.

I just sometimes need to let this truth set in and this always helps me. It is pretty rare these days that I get hung up on people hurting me or doing me wrong. I tend to feel a bit more disappointed than hurt. However, on the big hurts of my past, when I was in the heat of them, it was simply considering what Christ did for me that moved me along in the forgiving process. Jesus's last words to God…

Father forgive them-they know not what they do.

> **Consider the Choice:** Forgive as Jesus did, wiping away all the pain, and recourse that is accumulating as a result of this unforgiven.
>
> Evaluate and when applicable believe Jesus was right when he said they know not what they do.

Several years ago I had the fortunate opportunity to witness my daughter, Riley, come to Christ. She was around seven or eight, just understanding concrete thinking more deeply. We were packing up old books when we found an old family favorite entitled '*Emma & Mommy Talk to God,*' by Marianne Williamson, (January 24, 2006). We hadn't read it for a couple years, but she held it fondly and asked me to read it.

As I read, she kept asking me questions, and with each question her heartfelt words turned to hurt, sorrow, and more.

Riley: Why did Jesus do that?

My response: Because He loves us.

Riley: But he died. I thought He lived forever?

My response: Yes, he died here in this world, so we could ALL live forever.

Riley: Will you live forever?

*My response: Everyone will live forever **if** they truly understand and believe just what Christ did for them. But some don't believe.*

Riley: Why don't they believe?

My response: I think they have never been told.

Riley: We have to tell them.

My response: Yes, Baby we do.

Riley: (She stopped me from turning another page, and quietly began to cry) He did that for me?

My response: Yes, Baby, He did that for you.

With a truly touched heart... from that day on, she was His~

Children sometimes grasp it all better than us. She worried about the rest of the people in the world before herself. She worried about Jesus before them all. But, this is what our choice comes down to.

Consider the Choice: How can we accept what we cannot offer in return?

Do we only forgive others for our own health, to keep God close, to keep Satan away, to allow healing and peace alone? Or do we also forgive others for their sake, just as God in Christ did for us.

Here is a key I use to help others recognize when they ARE making a choice on forgiveness, whether they are aware of it or not.

Too often we think we are doing fine,
not resolvingor avoiding conflict or past hurts.

But when avoiding remember, as with all choices, we are always choosing whether we admit it or not. It is always a YES or a NO. Making an effort (working with God) to forgive is a yes, and doing nothing (metaphorically lying in B.E.D.) is a NO.

H.E.L.P. readiness on forgiveness

(When you're ready to turn to God for help)

H= Hurting Self: We've spoke a lot on how our thoughts in our heads are 'living' there. Bad thoughts are allowing the god of this world (Satan) into our minds while good thoughts invite God to dwell in us. Are you hurting yourself by letting Satan do His work in your life?

E= Emotional State: We truly can bring good to our lives by keeping good in our hearts... and vice versa.

> Consider the choice: What things do you find rolling around in your mind that are not noble, excellent, praiseworthy and all things good?
>
> Do you want these things to invite and entertain the devil in your house, your life?

"The good man out of the good treasure of his heart brings forth what is good; and the evil man out of the evil treasure brings forth what is evil; for his mouth speaks from that which fills his heart. Luke 6:45

Are you carrying around hurt, anger, jealousy, or pain for another in your heart? How do you think this is affecting your state?

L= Let Go: Do you keep going back to the same thing; same excuse (because my father did this I..., because I have this disease I..., because she did that I...) The freedom your life needs in order to grow is important, and I want everyone to be in this place. Remember the story of the woman who literally spent over 20 years trying to work through past male/female relationship pain, who one day turned TO God and found herself healed from it all. Now she is in a beautiful healthy marriage, reaping many rewards of this Godly place in her life.

P= Prove: Prove whether your priority is to be "right" or to break free of the foothold forgiveness has on you. You basically have to choose between one of the two options; and remember, by doing nothing you're choosing not to forgive.

Let what you say be simply 'Yes' or 'No'; anything more than this comes from evil. Matthew 5:37

You, my brothers and sisters, were called to be free. But do not use your freedom to indulge the sinful nature; rather, serve one another humbly in love. Galatians 5:13

"Are you choosing to not forgive someone of a past hurt?"

PART 6

A LEGACY DESIGNED FOR YOU

THE PROBLEM

CHAPTER 21
THAT THEY KNOW NOT

A LEGACY DESIGNED FOR YOU

A Legacy Designed for You

THE PROBLEM

THAT THEY KNOW NOT

Imagine that you have worked one place your entire life. And you're quite content with it. You work hard and are compensated well. There are hardships and dilemmas there, but you understand that this is much like life itself and you have grown accustomed to it. You have lived what you feel is a pretty successful life. Over the years you maybe thought about looking somewhere else once or twice, but you really didn't know where to start. Things were just fine, so you reminded yourself to be content. The idea dropped.

Then, because of a personal matter, you are required to move several states away and are pushed into getting a new job.

Your new job is amazing! Your coworkers are united, and each employee truly gives their all. The leadership teams are reputable. They lead by example, and are always striving to help you grow and excel. You are paid very well and are compensated with even more based on your performance. You are treated with respect and grace and expected to treat others the same. You are shocked and surprised at the level of contentment you settled for at your old job and with your old life... **as you had known nothing different.**

Consider the Problem:

- You could have stayed in your old job, missing out on growth, blessings, and fulfillment for no reason other than not knowing any different.
- Someone you care about might not know, when it comes to being accepted by Christ and all the joy that comes from walking in faith.
- Not everyone has a personal circumstance forcing them to make a change.

Are we keeping ourselves away for greatness?
When we surround our life with the same, we simply get more of the same. Do we surround ourselves with goodness and light? Do we as Christians go TO others or just stay WITH *our* people?

What if we try to help but they can't or wont hear us?
If they hear or listen, even a little, then go to them and speak, share, and hope. If they hear nothing or rebuke, then just love them in their presence and go to those who hear or will listen.

The next four and final chapters of this book (Part 6: A Legacy Designed For You) tell a similar story. A story of us not knowing what we do not know, a story of us accepting each day for what we have come to know, a story of us embracing all there is to know, and a story of us sharing what God wants everyone to know. We need to be clear on God's purpose for us, and what we are *not* doing, but *can* be doing.

We've spent the last 5 sections of this book covering, what I feel, is the legacy Jesus has left behind for us all. A legacy of unconditional love, hope for an eternal life for all, power that can take us places far beyond our own strength, a guide that lives and breathes in us, a map that shows us the way, peace that surpasses all understanding, and lastly, fulfillment which includes many blessings of the spirit and supply. All this is received with a heart that accepts it, and desires for God to be glorified by it!

I want each and every person to know, accept, embrace and share all God has to offer. Some folks I suppose closed this book long ago. Others, may never have moved past the coverlet. YOU made it to the end. To the inheritance! And I am so happy for you.

We started this book with the understanding that we are all in different places in our faith. Faith is faith, and in God's eyes we are either with Him or against Him. I know, with all my heart, that God simply wants us to be "LIVING" in our faith, growing in our faith. What I pray for, is that everyone I come into contact with will receive a nudge, desire, or intrigue to deepen their faith wherever they are at in life-and to have an undeniable need to infuse faith deeply into their day-to-day living. This is when relationships heal, we succeed in our work, fulfillment is gained, and health is restored. By doing this, I know that they will be abiding in 'The Living Legacy.'

How Is The Legacy Given?

By the Triune God

By God...

God is in, of, and above this world. He also lives and breathes in us. He is the truth and light. He is Love and all things good. We are His, and He *WANTS* to be ours.

God wants us to stay in the 'Word.' This is one way He stays in contact with us. These 'words,' when adopted, read, and embodied, become us. They transform our lives and as a result, our faith then grows more. Our relationship with God deepens, and we in turn, want to live and learn more, and so it goes on.

The Bible, God's living Word, is our gift and our map. It has every answer to our life issues, and includes everything God wants us to have and know. He leads us through these living words. The more we are in the 'Word,' the more it is in us...leading us and perfecting us.

God deeply desires a relationship with us. He wants us to go to church and warns us to avoid getting out of the habit of meeting together. So much of our faith is about relationships with 'thy neighbor,' spurring each other, singing, praying and learning together. We lead others to Him and through Him, by these loving and kind relationships.

By the Holy Spirit...

The Holy Spirit is our friend, and lives in us always. We can shut the Holy Spirit out, or listen carefully. We can respond to promptings, or ignore them. We can recognize the Holy Spirit's work in us and give God the glory, or we can write it off to coincidence and chance, giving the world God's credit.

It is often the Holy Spirit that can nudge a God-loving nonbeliever to Christ by muffling out this loud world enough for them to find Christ through the leading of this great Spirit. The Holy Spirit spurs and stirs in us enough to help us forgive more, love deeper, learn more, and embrace more. The Holy Spirit knows all things right and wrong. The Holy Spirit does not judge.

By Jesus Christ...

Jesus is our Savior who gave up His life for our life. Who loves us unconditionally and far more than we could image. He changed religion for us, making it two-fold. It is no longer of 'works' alone.

First, as a Christian, there is no doubt, and no gamble necessary over our eternity...we know **at the very moment** we give ourselves up to the Lord, with Jesus as our savior, that it is done.

The second, with this knowledge of what Jesus did for us comes complete ownership and accountability for receiving SUCH an insurmountable gift. Eternal life--- known now!

The Legacy Jesus left was the end...
And the beginning...
And binding!

The 'Living Legacy' is one of hope and a testament of faith. I believe Jesus, our Lord and Savior, left this for whosoever believes when He died and rose again.

I believe this story, the Jesus legacy left behind for each of us, is found in the pages of John 13-16. As Jesus had his last supper with the disciples, knowing He was leaving, he spent time affirming to them who He was, what his purpose was, what our purpose shall be, when his time was, when our time will be, where he was going, and how or when we would ever get there.

The Living Legacy
A Faith-infused place in this world,
between here & there!

The Living Legacy: (Left behind for us.) It is one of love, hope, power, guidance, peace, and provider, carried out by the Father, the Son and the Holy Spirit.

The Will: Which is the Bible, 'God's will' written out for all to review, including a multitude of gifts waiting to be claimed by our acceptance, causing the black and white words to take life in us.

The Contract: Already binding, with the blood of Jesus between God, the Holy Spirit, Jesus and ...

whosoever believes

THE WORD

CHAPTER 22

THAT THE "WORD" IS THE LIVING LEGACY OF CHRIST

A LEGACY DESIGNED FOR YOU

A Legacy Designed for You

THE WORD

THAT THE "WORD" IS THE LIVING LEGACY OF CHRIST

L egacy
noun, plural **legacies.**
1. *Law.* a gift of property, especially personal property, as money, by will; a bequest.
2. Anything handed down from the past, as from an ancestor or predecessor: *the legacy of ancient Rome.*

While in 'The Word' chapter of *A Legacy Designed For You*, we will be looking at some impactful, God breathed words, straight from the Bible regarding the Holy Spirt, wisdom, Jesus, faith, and the 'Word' which I hope will spark an engulfing flame of truth and light for all who read this.

FAITH

If we know the legacy of Jesus is left for those who believe and have faith, we need to keep it, and we need to always grow in our faith...

Now faith is confidence in what we hope for and assurance about what we do not see. Hebrews 11:1

*For it is by grace you have been saved, through faith—and this is not from yourselves, it is the gift of God—*Ephesians 2:8

so that your faith might not rest on human wisdom, but on God's power. 1 Corinthians 2:5

Trust in the LORD with all thine heart; and lean not unto thine own understanding. Proverbs 3:5-6

Consequently, faith comes from hearing the message, and the message is heard through the word about Christ. Romans 10:17

THE WORD

We know the Bible is one of our most amazing gifts left behind, and I pray that throughout this book you have been touched by its wisdom and all it has to offer. If you were a seeker of the 'Word' already, I am in awe of your discipline and true insight that I know you have already gained by the inevitable wisdom that is growing in you.

> **Consider the word:** You understand the 'Word' and how it works and lives in you because you believe (you have the spirit of truth in you). What about the nonbeliever? How will they ever come if we do not do our part?

Above all, you must understand that in the last days scoffers will come, scoffing and following their own evil desires. They will say, "Where is this 'coming' he promised? Ever since our ancestors died, everything goes on as it has since the beginning of creation. 2 Peter 3:3-4

All Scripture is God-breathed and is useful for teaching, rebuking, correcting and training in righteousness, so that the servant of God may be thoroughly equipped for every good work. 2 Timothy 3:16-17

For the word of God is alive and active. Sharper than any double-edged sword, it penetrates even to dividing soul and spirit, joints and marrow; it judges the thoughts and attitudes of the heart. Hebrews 4:12

Until I come, devote yourself to the public reading of Scripture, to exhortation, to preaching and to teaching. 1 Timothy 4:13

If you remain in me and my words remain in you, ask whatever you wish, and it will be done for you. John 15:7

So Jesus said to the Jews who had believed in him, "If you abide in my word, you are truly my disciples, John 8:31 ESV

WISDOM

The world cannot accept Him, because it neither sees Him nor knows Him. But you know Him, for He lives with you and will be in you. I will not leave you as orphans; I will come to you. Before long, the world will not see me anymore, but you will see me. Because I live, you also will live. On that day you will realize that I am in my Father, and you are in me, and I am in you. John 14:17-20

See to it that no one takes you captive through hollow and deceptive philosophy, which depends on human tradition and the elemental spiritual forces[a] of this world rather than on Christ. Colossians 2:8

I found many worldly and 'universal' approaches used by health and wellness experts out there. I feel very called

to stay clear of these approaches. I want to lead, coach, teach, and inspire with a holistic approach that is clearly Christian in philosophy, and true to the Word.

If any of you lacks wisdom, you should ask God, who gives generously to all without finding fault, and it will be given to you. James 1:5

For this reason they could not believe, because, as Isaiah says elsewhere: "He has blinded their eyes and hardened their hearts, so they can neither see with their eyes, nor understand with their hearts, nor turn—and I would heal them." John 12:39-40

The mind governed by the flesh is hostile to God; it does not submit to God's law, nor can it do so. Those who are in the realm of the flesh cannot please God. Romans 8:7-8

And even if our gospel is veiled, it is veiled to those who are perishing. The god of this age has blinded the minds of unbelievers, so that they cannot see the light of the gospel that displays the glory of Christ, who is the image of God.

2 Corinthians 4:3-4

For the message of the cross is foolishness to those who are perishing, but to us who are being saved it is the power of God. For it is written: "I will destroy the wisdom of the wise; the intelligence of the intelligent I will frustrate." 1 Corinthians 1:18-19

Furthermore, just as they did not think it worthwhile to retain the knowledge of God, so God gave them over to a depraved mind, so that they do what ought not to be done. They have become filled with every kind of wickedness, evil, greed and depravity. They are full of envy, murder, strife, deceit and malice. They are gossips, slanderers, God-haters, insolent, arrogant and boastful; they invent ways of doing evil; they disobey their parents; they have no understanding, no fidelity, no love, no mercy. Although they know God's righteous decree that those who do such things deserve death, they not only continue to do these very things but also approve of those who practice them. Romans 1:28-32

HOLY SPIRIT

The person without the Spirit does not accept the things that come from the Spirit of God but considers them foolishness, and cannot understand them because they are discerned only through the Spirit. 1 Corinthians 2:14

They said to you, "In the last times there will be scoffers who will follow their own ungodly desires." These are the people who divide you, who follow mere natural instincts and do not have the Spirit. Jude 1:18-19

Sometimes people think it is weird to talk about how the Holy Spirit or God worked in them, fearing others might think they are strange or making it up. But there is so much to gain by sharing your faith through these stories.

Consider the Word: The separation of believers and nonbelievers is widening. There are more people now who truly feel religion, and leaning on God, is weak, idealistic and/or strange. Remember that it is you who knows. Truly knowing is to respond to this in faith...and go make believers.

One of the most amazing and non-contestable acts of faith I have ever been a part of happened to me years ago.

• • •

I was the director of nursing at the time for a long term care center. I had gone back to work one night after supper, which was not a usual occurrence. However, while I was there, a patient of ours nearly died. I had been available at just the right time and he ended up regaining his breathing.

As he got his breath and bearings back, he looked me straight in the eyes and said thank you in very garbled speech. My heart broke for him. To be honest, my instincts just kicked in and part of me, after he started breathing again, wondered if I hadn't been there maybe he could have or would have been able to move on to an eternal life of no more pain and suffering.

He was a lovely man with a positive outlook on life regardless of his circumstances. I truly loved him. He really didn't live much past that. His family was around him in his last days providing a vigil of love, and I slowly forgot of my wonders about intervening as I did.

One Saturday morning my sister and mom picked me up to go garage sale hunting. I sat in the back seat perched in the middle leaning forward so we could all talk. At some point I must have gotten quiet and my mom asked what was wrong.

I remember saying 'nothing.' But I went on to tell them of how odd it was that I had thought of this sweet little patient of mine, how I had stepped in and probably extended his life by a few weeks. I thought maybe that was bothering me. Then I told them I thought it had more to do with his family. They were so supportive-even though I had a twinge of uncertainty about intervening and postponing what I knew would be his Glory, he at least had an amazing family who showered him with love, almost a vigil they gave him in these last days...that must have been it, I told them. And I put it out of my mind. I remember 'poo-pooing' in it and looking at the digital clock in front of me trying to focus my mind back in the present... 9:37, we were doing good with time and should be able to hit a few sales.

I must have gotten quiet again. My mom asked me once more if I was still thinking about this patient. I respectfully said, "nooo?" and then I told them I felt like he said thank you to me. Like he was affirmed of this time he had as good and I needed to know that instead of feeling poorly about anything. I thought surely I was going crazy, and decided to move on before they both thought I was as well.

All this sounds okay, a little odd I know, but then...

On Monday morning as I was going through my weekend paperwork and reports, I found a death certificate on my desk for 9:37 Saturday morning.

He most definitely said goodbye and thank you!

Without a doubt I know the Holy Spirit lives in us and moves through us. We need to know this, believe this, and use this.

> **Consider the Word:** Those without the Spirit do not accept things of the Spirit.
>
> If you are alone journaling or are in a study group, consider sharing stories that up until now you have not even let yourself believe is or was the Holy Spirit. Sharing your faith helps others know this too...this is one reason why the Word is full of stories.

JESUS

Matthew 12:50 For whoever does the will of my Father in heaven is my brother and sister and mother."

Matthew 4:19 "Come, follow me," Jesus said, "and I will send you out to fish for people."

"No one, sir," she said. "Then neither do I condemn you," Jesus declared. "Go now and leave your life of sin." When Jesus spoke again to the people, he said, "I am the light of the world. Whoever follows me will never walk in darkness, but will have the light of life." John 8:11-12

THE PURPOSE OF THE LEGACY

The thief comes only to steal and kill and destroy. I came that they may have life and have it abundantly. John 10:10 ESV

Now to him who is able to do far more abundantly than all that we ask or think, according to the power at work within us, Ephesians 3:20 ESV

Command those who are rich in this present world not to be arrogant nor to put their hope in wealth, which is so uncertain, but to put their hope in God, who richly provides us with everything for our enjoyment. 1 Timothy 6:17

Consider the Gift: Riches;

Be wise to keep your trust within your Father, never falling prey to the joys of uncertain riches

---

For this people's heart has become calloused; they hardly hear with their ears, and they have closed their eyes. Otherwise they might see with their eyes, hear with their ears, understand with their hearts and turn, and I would heal them.' But blessed are your eyes because they see, and your ears because they hear. Matthew 13:15-16

What specifically does John 13-16 tell us about the legacy Jesus left behind, and how does that relate to us and our purpose?

Let's read John 13-16. We will dive into these verses a bit deeper in the Consider the Choice Chapter but for now pay particular attention to a few key points. It is the night before Jesus will be crucified, and He knows that He will be leaving the disciples and His physical place with them. He knows why

He will be leaving, that they will not be able to come, that He will be leaving the living word *in them to record* for us all, that the Holy Spirit will then take His place in the world for us, and that we will still be cared for, protected, loved and guided by God, the three-in-one.

After looking again at Jesus's last hours on this land, I hope you can see how He truly wanted to leave us with a purpose. He lived a life and legacy of true compassion and commitment to love and serve God. He left us all our gifts with one purpose; to go and serve in a loving way.

We are to carry on this legacy. We are NOT to get hung up on where we are in life, because that is the wonderful blessing about being a Christian-we don't qualify or deserve this love… or this mission.

We simply need to love and be loved… believe and make believers.

THE GIFT

CHAPTER 23
THAT HE BE GLORIFIED

A LEGACY DESIGNED FOR YOU

A Legacy Designed for You

THE GIFT

THAT HE BE GLORIFIED

A great way to follow up our close look at John 13-16 and what Jesus left for us, is to actually see how this Living Legacy of Jesus may transform our lives. This chapter is designed to help you see the significance of infusing faith deeply into your day-to-day life, to set goals that are consistent with your God-given life purpose, and where God is not only in line with these goals, but He is actually your driving force.

These Goals work together for the good of self and others. They depend on each other, and are not self-seeking but rather sacredly-serving. As far back as I can remember, I have had a heart for helping others to be their best version of themselves. This worked very well for me while leading nurses, and while caring for patients who needed to reach life sustaining goals. I simply want for us all to do what we are supposed to be doing and to do our best.

As I started coaching, this same passion rang true, but now I am in my own practice. I am able to speak more openly about what I feel is the key to living our life purpose with true success.

How to Get My Life Purpose Working and In Sync

This occurs when we put 'Living' at the top of all we do!

Living with God, the Spirit, and Jesus as your Savior, truly does have you 'Living' life to the fullest. I have been helping others reach their career goals, health goals, and personal goals for over twenty years, and without passion and a driving force, it is near impossible.

When our driving force is the omniscient, omnipotent, and omnipresent one, we find ourselves in a place where we are making things happen and...

GOD RIGHTLY GETS THE GLORY!

Life Purpose
Glorifies God ~ Bears Fruit ~ Serves Others

The 'Living' Legacy: Faith-Infused Living!

The Living Legacy: (left behind for us all) It is a life of love, hope, power, guidance, peace and provision. A legacy of unconditional love, hope for an eternal life for all, power that can take us places far beyond our own strength, a guide that lives and breathes in us, a map that shows us the way, peace that surpasses all understanding, and lastly, fulfillment which includes many blessings of the Spirit. All of this is received with a heart that accepts it and desires for God to be glorified by it!

Fulfill Your Legacy's philosophy is based around the foundation of four legacies: The Living Legacy being the core and starting place...the corner stone. I have included many of Fulfill Your Legacy's tools and aides in this book for you to begin your plan for deeply infusing faith into you daily life, and for setting God-assisted goals that you feel confident God has aligned for you. These specific items I use to work with my clients can also help you begin your journey of abiding in Jesus's Legacy!

Try using these steps to get started on your life purpose journey

1. Tackle specific areas of weakness. (Try looking to the "S" Study Yourself section from your sweet spot experiment to get yourself started on a good list. And journal, you'll appreciate having done this later.)

2. Use God to help transform weaknesses into stepping stones for success. *(I have many tools to do this, and use whichever is best for any given client, but think about how you have best learned in the past. With encouragement? Tough love? Also find a mentor in the area of your weakness, use them, and return the favor.)*

3. Match up worldly strengths, God-given talents, and passions to consider just where God is calling you. *(Also from the 'sweet spot.')*

4. Assess overall health and well-being, making sure to align goals up with optimal health. From weight and exercise, to career changes and life transitions. Keeping a healthy balance in all areas of your life is essential. *(You can't have one area of your life literally sucking the energy out of you and expect the rest of your being to be untouched. We need to find ways to have you working at your best place in all areas so consider some health goals, work goals, etc.)*

5. Use the 4-step model of consider the problem, consider the Word, consider the gifts, and consider the choice to make some of the best goals you have ever had work. *(This is such a life changing way of living. Honestly, if you take all problems and do this...it will send the devil running with a backpack full of your stress, anxiety, energy and despair. It will teach you to call on and depend on the Almighty who has SO much power just waiting to use on you, His beloved.)*

6. Day by day I watch people transform and embrace the life God has called them to live. And we lift up our

praises as I commend them with a job well done. They give God the glory, and we wait to see how they will be blessed with even more! *Giving God the glory is the easy part; but remember that if you didn't work as for the Lord while trying to live your purpose, then it is not exactly His Glory. Make sure day by day you pray and diligently work to serve the Lord and then as the blessings come, give God that glory!*

7. Learn how to use the blessings of God wisely, and even more as they multiply, and then do more…AND SO IT GOES! *(Pray on this and plan ahead, be disciplined. Give graciously of service, money, heart and trust.)*

The other Legacy programs are the Loving Legacy, Learning Legacy, and Leading Legacy. These are designed to work together knowing that first getting a strong foundation of faith-filled living is crucial. It is what God has called us to do, and we will be living examples of Christ by doing so!

In the same way, let your light shine before others, that they may see your good deeds and glorify your Father in heaven. Matthew 5:16

THE CHOICE

CHAPTER 24

THAT ALL THIS IS YOURS "IF YOU..."

A LEGACY DESIGNED FOR YOU

A Legacy Designed for You

THE CHOICE

THAT ALL THIS IS YOURS, "IF YOU..."

If you...
I went through John 13, 14, 15 and 16 NIV looking for just how many times Jesus says to the disciples, "If you..." "If you belong to me." "If you know me." "If you love me." "If you remain in me." "If you keep me."

In this final chapter, **we will review what Jesus says he will leave behind for us, how it relates to the previous chapters we have studied,** and how all this leads us to our life purpose. There is only one way to eternal life and many ways to remain in his blessings.

So let's take a look at just what it is we are choosing or not choosing through our insight and actions...

YOU ARE HIS & HE IS YOURS

ADOPTED BY CHRIST: "IF YOU" BELONG TO ME

Here we came to understand that it isn't until we own the fact that we ARE God's children, where we are His, and He is ours, that we are able to own all that God, Christ, and the Holy Spirit have to offer. Not until we truly love God is

He truly in us and able to work in us, give us insight beyond simply hearing words or reading black and white letters. We actually need to let Him in, own Him, and be adopted to truly embrace all He is.

We are then part of Him. And where He is, so will we be. In John 14 Jesus is reassuring us for when he leaves, that regardless of how alone we may feel here in this world, rest assured, we are NEVER alone. There will always be a place for us with Him in heaven.

> *"Do not let your hearts be troubled. You believe in God[a]; believe also in me. My Father's house has many rooms; if that were not so, would I have told you that I am going there to prepare a place for you? And if I go and prepare a place for you, I will come back and take you to be with me that you also may be where I am. You know the way to the place where I am going."* John 14:1-4

- **Assurance…. you are accepted into eternal life NOW:**

If we want to know we are accepted into God's house right here and now, there is only one way.

Accept that this verse, John 14:6-7, as true!

Christianity is the only organized faith that doesn't work off works. We still work for the Lord, but once we "give" ourselves to Christ, we now do work for God out of accountability and as a result of immense insight and gratitude gained by this oneness.

> *Jesus answered, "I am the way and the truth and the life. No one comes to the Father except through me.* ***If you really know me,*** *you will know my Father as well. From now on, you do know him and have seen him."* John 14:6-7

- **Jesus tells us "HOW" we will get there…stay in God!**

"Now remain in my love." We are instructed to remain in the 'good' place we find ourselves in right after we give ourselves to Christ. Jesus and God knew the 'good' place the disciples

were in when they were walking 'with' Jesus. Soon they would need to be spreading the Word without his physical presence. So Jesus left the disciples an understanding of how to keep working in and of him, and of his promise of eternal life, and how they could get back to him when their time here on earth was done.

This is how it will work for us too. We need to keep Jesus, God, and the Holy Spirit in and of us.

They are the way back to the Father when our days here are done.

"As the Father has loved me, so have I loved you. Now remain in my love. John 15:9

In that day you will ask in my name. I am not saying that I will ask the Father on your behalf. No, the Father himself loves you because you have loved me and have believed that I came from God. I came from the Father and entered the world; now I am leaving the world and going back to the Father." John 16:26-28

PERFECTLY IMPERFECT

Not one of us is holy perfect…. or as magnificent as the Father. There is no comparing in God's eyes. Only He can see us with eyes that love unconditionally (making no one better than the next). He knows everything we have done, are doing, and will do; and He still loves us.

He made us into who we are from before we were formed, to our last breath. He expects that we love as Jesus taught us, and reassures us that we will be rewarded with blessings as we do so. We will recognize, as God's blessings are bestowed upon us, that these are in fact a result of our good work. But not because of our good work. When all this is done in and of God, it is He who deserves the glory.

- **An Example of what He asks of us, to love each other:**
  *When he had finished washing their feet, he put on his clothes and returned to his place. "Do you understand what I have done for you?" he asked them. "You call me 'Teacher' and 'Lord,' and rightly so, for that is what I am. Now that I, your Lord and Teacher, have washed your feet, you also should wash one another's feet. I have set you an example that you should do as I have done for you. Very truly I tell you, no servant is greater than his master, nor is a messenger greater than the one who sent him. Now that you know these things, you will be blessed **if you do them**.* John 13:12-17

- **Being in and of God will help perfect us.**
  Staying in footholds of past hurts, setbacks, and pain keeps us from God. And from growing and doing God's work, and from His blessings.
  *"I am the true vine, and my Father is the gardener. He cuts off every branch in me that bears no fruit, while every branch that does bear fruit he prunes[a] so that it will be even more fruitful. You are already clean because of the word I have spoken to you. Remain in me, as I also remain in you. No branch can bear fruit by itself; it must remain in the vine. Neither can you bear fruit **unless you remain in me**.* John 15:1-4

WISE CHOICES WORK

The Triune God, if we accept one, we need to take them all: We should not have one without the other. This isn't true acceptance and doesn't assure our salvation then. (Think on that. God alone is lovely…but that doesn't assure our salvation.)

*Very truly I tell you, whoever accepts anyone I send accepts me; and **whoever accepts me** accepts the one who sent me."*
John 13:20

Accountability, we CHOOSE to do good.

We do not HAVE to be perfect to get to heaven. It is not by our works alone. Yet, out of this oneness (accepting the Triune), our heart's desire with all we have, to do good work.

*Very truly I tell you, **whoever believes** in me will do the works I have been doing, and they will do even greater things than these, because I am going to the Father.* John 14:12

- **Thank you Jesus for the Holy Spirit, in the here and now, helping us make wise choices.**
  The Holy Spirit, the advocate, compels and helps us to do 'good' work, (God's work). We are so gifted to have this. He leads us, helps us discern, and to make wise decisions.

But very truly I tell you, it is for your good that I am going away. Unless I go away, the Advocate will not come to you; but if I go, I will send him to you. When he comes, he will prove the world to be in the wrong about sin and righteousness and judgment: John 16:7-8

MISTAKES MATTER

THE HOLY SPIRIT WILL TEACH US ALL THINGS:
Again, we are so blessed to have the Holy Spirit with us, but not everyone has this gift. Sharing this belief with our neighbors as they fall short shows compassion and acceptance. Finding Jesus can be hard for nonbelievers. We need to love-in a little light into the hearts of nonbelievers-It will grow from there. God is love and the Holy Spirit is God. This is how we can one by one make believers of all.
"*If you love me, keep my commands. And I will ask the Father, and he will give you another advocate to help you and be with you forever—the Spirit of truth. The world cannot accept him, because it neither sees him nor knows*

239

him. But you know him, for he lives with you and will be in you. John 14:15-17

- **Christians have the gift of the Triune help always.** As long as we keep Jesus in our hearts always, we have access to the Triune always. We are growing with the help of the Triune God. Even while falling and experiencing setbacks, they proceed us further. We can count on them to straighten our paths when we fall short and protect us from harm with each mistake. At times we will have overwhelming life circumstances and it will be them that pulls us through and offers us peace. We love and need the Triune God for real physical and spiritual growth.

But the Advocate, the Holy Spirit, whom the Father will send in my name, will teach you all things and will remind you of everything I have said to you. John 14:26

FORGIVENESS FULFILLS

WE ARE FORGIVEN OUT OF LOVE, ACCEPTED SINFUL BEINGS:

*"A new command I give you: Love one another. As I have loved you, so you must love one another. By this everyone will know that you are my disciples, **if you love one another.***"
John 13:34-35

A LEGACY DESIGNED FOR YOU

LEGACY OF OBEYING GOD:

You will do even greater things with the Holy Spirit's help, with the Father's power and support, and with Christ's love and acceptance.

The words I say to you I do not speak on my own authority. Rather, it is the Father, living in me, who is doing his work. Believe me when I say that I am in the Father and *the Father is in me; or at least believe on the evidence of the works themselves. Very truly I tell you, **whoever believes in me** will do the works I have been doing, and they will do even greater things than these, because I am going to the Father. And I will do whatever you ask in my name, so that the Father may be glorified in the Son. You may ask me for anything in my name, and I will do it.* John 14:10-14

- **Legacy of peace, freedom of fear and anxiety:**

Peace I leave with you; my peace I give you. I do not give to you as the world gives. Do not let your hearts be troubled and do not be afraid. John 14:27

- **Legacy of generosity & supply: "IF YOU"** remain in me…

*"I am the vine; you are the branches. **If you remain in me** and I in you, you will bear much fruit; apart from me you can do nothing. **If you do not remain in me,** you are like a branch that is thrown away and withers; such branches are picked up, thrown into the fire and burned. **If you remain in me** and my words remain in you, ask whatever you wish, and it will be done for you. This is to my Father's glory, that you bear much fruit, showing yourselves to be my disciples.* John 15:5-8

- **Legacy of loving:**

*"As the Father has loved me, so have I loved you. Now remain in my love. **If you keep my commands,** you will remain in my love, just as I have kept my Father's commands and remain in his love. I have told you this so that my joy may be in you and that your joy may be complete. My command is this: Love each other as I have loved you.* John 15:9-12

- **Legacy of provider:**

You did not choose me, but I chose you and appointed you so that you might go and bear fruit—fruit that will last—and so that whatever you ask in my name *the Father will give you.* John 15:16

- **Legacy of strong heritage:**

If you belonged to the world, it would love you as its own. As it is, you do not belong to the world, but I have chosen you out of the world. That is why the world hates you. John 15:19

- **Legacy of joyfulness:**

…Very truly I tell you, my Father will give you whatever you ask in my name. Until now you have not asked for anything in my name. Ask and you will receive, and your joy will be complete. John 16:23-24

- **Legacy of peace:**

"I have told you these things, so that in me you may have peace. In this world you will have trouble. But take heart! I have overcome the world." John 16:33

THIS IS MY COMMAND

As I read of the legacy Jesus left for each of us, written in John 13-16 over and over, I am in awe of just how simple such an amazing and complete gift can be.

For all we are given, with Christ as our Savior, we are simply asked to LOVE…

"A new command I give you: Love one another. As I have loved you, so you must love one another. By this everyone

will know that you are my disciples, if you love one another."
John 13:34-35

My command is this: Love each other as I have loved you.
John 15:12

This is my command: Love each other. John 15:17

END NOTES

I AM HIS AND HE IS MINE/The Gift
Monty Roberts, "Join-Up," http://www.montyroberts.com/ab_about_monty/ju_about/, accessed August 30, 2016
Julia Child, Wikipedia, https://en.wikipedia.org/wiki/Julia_Child, accessed August 30, 2016

PERFECTLY IMPERFECT/The Choice
Branden Heath, "Give Me Your Eyes," https://www.youtube.com/watch?v=P5AkNqLuVgY , accessed August 30, 2016

WISE CHOICES WORK/The Problem
Historical Religious Demographics of the United states, Wikipedia, https://en.wikipedia.org/wiki/History_of_religion_in_the_United_States#Demographics , accessed August 30, 2016
Analysis Paralysis, Wikipedia, https://en.wikipedia.org/wiki/Analysis_paralysis , accessed August 30, 2016

WISE CHOICES WORK/The Gift
Stephen Baldwin, Testimony https://www.youtube.com/watch?v=QGpFqmi_28U, accessed August 30, 2016

FORGIVENESS FULFILLS/The Problem
Rich Cavaness, "The Emotional and Physical Effects of Not Forgiving," Tuesday, 07 May 2013 Health and Wellness, http://theroadadventure.org/blog/entry/the-emotional-and-physical-effects-of-not-forgiving, accessed August 30, 2016

FORGIVENESS FULFILLS/The Word
Joyce Meyer, *Do Yourself a Favor... Forgive*, (FaithWords; 1 edition, April 3, 2012)

TAKE CONTROL OF YOUR FUTURE

Join the Living Legacy Leaders

Imagine **Awaking**…to the **Legacy** left behind for you!

➢ Imagine finding your individual PURPOSE in life and learning how to run with it.
➢ Imagine having applicable steps for gaining HEALTH and wellness that sustains & nurtures continued strength, growth, and prosperity.
➢ Imagine learning how to tap into PEACE, JOY, LOVE and BLESSINGS that will carry you throughout your days.

The Living Legacy training is a powerful experience that has led so many to their true potential and life fulfillment! Individuals and groups from all around the world have been through the powerful transformation of Fulfill Your Legacy coaching and the processes highlighted in *Awaking the Living Legacy.*

Participants can join from anywhere in the world.

FIND OUT MORE AT
nicciekliegl.com

What's the cost of not embracing all that awaits you?

Join us at the
AWAKING THE LIVING LEGACY

Live Event

Imagine attending the *'Awaking the Living Legacy'* training in a live summit! Each spring Niccie passionately opens the doors of her community to those ready for life changing impact!

"That the God of our Lord Jesus Christ, the Father of glory, may give you the Spirit of wisdom and of revelation in the knowledge of him, having the eyes of your hearts enlightened, that you may know what is the hope to which he has called you, what are the riches of his glorious inheritance in the saints."
Ephesians 1:17-18

FIND OUT MORE AT
nicciekliegl.com

CPSIA information can be obtained
at www.ICGtesting.com
Printed in the USA
FFOW02n1614141017
41003FF